Indigokro

Indigokro

BARE BONES:
A COLLECTION OF POEMS
1989-2016

Indigokro

BALBOA.
PRESS
A DIVISION OF HAY HOUSE

Balboa Press books may be ordered through booksellers or by contacting:

Balboa Press
A Division of Hay House
1663 Liberty Drive
Bloomington, IN 47403
www.balboapress.com
1 (877) 407-4847

Because of the dynamic nature of the Internet, any web addresses or links contained in this book may have changed since publication and may no longer be valid. The views expressed in this work are solely those of the author and do not necessarily reflect the views of the publisher, and the publisher hereby disclaims any responsibility for them.

The author of this book does not dispense medical advice or prescribe the use of any technique as a form of treatment for physical, emotional, or medical problems without the advice of a physician, either directly or indirectly. The intent of the author is only to offer information of a general nature to help you in your quest for emotional and spiritual well-being. In the event you use any of the information in this book for yourself, which is your constitutional right, the author and the publisher assume no responsibility for your actions.

Any people depicted in stock imagery provided by Thinkstock are models, and such images are being used for illustrative purposes only.
Certain stock imagery © Thinkstock.

Print information available on the last page.

ISBN: 978-1-5043-6112-5 (sc)
ISBN: 978-1-5043-6114-9 (hc)
ISBN: 978-1-5043-6113-2 (e)

Library of Congress Control Number: 2016910812

Balboa Press rev. date: 07/19/2016

I dedicate my first book to Lynnie Frederick, who discovered me and my writings. Without her, you would not be reading this now.

Contents

Introduction...xi

Life Is a Circle I

Dusk in Time 3

Pie in the Window 5

Bare Bones 7

He Was Here 8

What Love?..9

Amanuensis.. 10

The Many Are One.. 11

Thoughts into Words.. 14

Two Hands.. 16

Let It Rain... 18

In Memory 20

Marriage of the Heart 22

Bury Me without the Key 24

Not Just Another Fish 26

What Was After All.. 30

Silence Is Calling 31

More than Dirt 33

One Rose 35

A Moment of Intent... 36

Let the Eye Follow Itself 39

I'm Not You 40

House of Sorrow.. 42

Make Your Stand 44

Need to Be Needed 46

Serenity Significance... 48

Falling.. 51

The Old Evil Eye 52

Was There 55

Bound by What's Up 56

I Will Awake... 58

For Every Poet 59
To Fall Prey.. 62
In the Presence of Contrast 63
Within All of Me 65
Where We Are Lead Now 66
No One Ever Told You 68
Unconventional Vision.. 70
No Interruptions 72
Wandering Away, Dream Relief....................................... 73
Love Is Always Worth the Risk.. 76
Flesh and Blood.. 77
The Eternal Stare 79
Open Message 81
In the Living Heart of One Open Eye 84
Falling for You.. 85
All Our Outlets 87
West Park Street 89
Lone Soldier... 91
Every Direction by Twilight... 93
The Reliable One 95
Food for Thought... 96
When Love Is Gone.. 97
Than I Ever Been... 99
The Prince of Wealth to Be 101
Behind the Curtain... 104
Spirit of Light.. 109
Over There Is Here 110
Many Untold Stories 111
The Missing Piece 113
What Will Be Is Already.. 115
Innocent Blood... 116
The Source 118
Calm 120
Frozen in Time 121
Once... 122
Mr. Home-Wrecker... 123

Forget Me Not 125

The Basement Boy 126

Living Her Land of Milk and Honey 128

Forgive and Forget 131

Dust of the Earth 133

When You're Not Ready 134

No Longer Break 137

All I Got 138

He Was Just Here 139

"They Are You" 141

Angel in the Night 143

The Place Is You 145

Awakening 147

Unturned 149

Take Myself as I Am Now 150

Ancient Vision 151

Set Yourself Free 153

Clueless Reality 154

By the Old Moonlight Window 156

Visions of Power 158

None Greater 160

Ageless Conquest 161

Vague 163

My Loving Darkness 164

Not So Fast 166

Everything Is Good Laying Down 168

Down the Hall 170

Down and Out the Side Door 172

You Can Stay 176

The Magnifier 177

A Christmas Eve Night 178

Twentieth-Century Indian Upbringing 180

The Transition 182

Wake Up and Go to Sleep 183

Before I Was Born 185

Broken Sheep 186

Left Unattended..188

Another Train..190

Facing the No End..192

All that Can Be Was Put in Me.......................................193

The Visitors...194

Into the Other Side..195

Paradigm...196

If and When...197

Love Is...198

Open up to the Night...199

Dwell Upon the Well and See...201

Earth and Sky...202

The Sign of the Cross...204

Twilight Silence Speaks..206

All the Same..207

By Dripping Candle Lights..208

Nobody Knows...210

To the Point..211

To Do and Not Know..212

I'll Be Right Back...213

What You Don't Know Can Teach You...........................215

You Are Heaven..216

Too Good to Be True..217

I Am Sure..218

What Does It Feel Like...220

Stays a Bit...221

Endless Muddy Trails...222

Love Is the Disguise...225

When the Breathless Still Mind Leaves..........................228

Steep Deep Slowly All over Hearts.................................230

The Unrealized, Noticed..232

The Prayer...233

Hitting the Mark..234

Now above It...235

Introduction

It was a progression of spilling words out onto paper and then tossing them into a cardboard box tucked away in the corner of the closet. Years of logging and unloading were unknowingly the antidote, and this was sowing the seeds while he was exploring his innermost depths.

And the universe is your eternal ink well,
and as you dip your mind
into it as a quill—

He thought to himself in a spirit dialogue the question, "What am I going to do with all of those writings and compositions?" Then a direct, sincere insight revealed back to him, "Wait twenty-five years, and then you will know what to do with them."

Your words are the words
of the power of your birth
and everyone's birth.
You are pregnant with
the meanings.
Only they will reveal—

This collection of poems is comprised of and derives from many of his life experiences and from an unrepressed, expansive workmanship of artistries.

You can only touch
What your senses can't reveal
Because only under the surface
Is where I am real.
My life is parallel to yours.
You'll find out when you open doors.
Lead your imagination

To the garden of your mind,
And you'll stop denying
What it is you need to find.

It's when the beautiful turn ugly and the terrible turn wonderful. When memory and amnesia make up and there's peace. When that "something greater" than your beliefs, fears and religion steps in without any prayers, faith, or love to ignite it all. It was just "being," sometimes just being still or quiet would break the ice in connecting with the higher self.

Kevin Oswald
Indigokro

Life Is a Circle

Eyes that smile from past memories,
Visions that dreamers dream across the seas:
Falling stars, rainbows, autumn trees
Give birth again to newborn ease.

The skies do always cloud with gray
In the midst of harvest and its day.
Heavenly raindrops paint the leaves
As all of nature whispers on its knees.

In tender red, gold, orange, and brown,
Slowly falling, whirling round and round,
Ancient winds make these bound
Till they lightly lie on ground.

Then they skip, twist, crackle in October winds,
Preparing all of creation before winter begins.
The beauty of earth is what we see;
It's one of life's grandest scenery.

The smell of woods in cool, crisp air,
Dodging, dancing around every mountain and stream—
The artist of glory has come to share
Fall's dazzling colors of inner pageantry.

As the season ends, she slowly settles in
Like stillness when all is white,
Hiding out till winter's flight:
Another new moment begins its life.

Antique chairs, quiet in nothingness;
Green plants grow beside them in single dress.
Windows feed with warmth and light
Till cold and dark comes starry night.

I wander like a ghost from the past
Into the quiet living room,
Looking back how all has passed,
Now gazing up to yonder moon.

Moving through the stillness
Where moonlight is given by the sun
Till morning comes dawning—
Another night is done.

Thawing rivers crack, break again;
Spirit of change guards like a friend,
Breathing a sigh of relief,
Reminding me of color's tender leaf.

Dusk in Time

My thoughts swarm like dragonflies
Above the gentle pond
Beneath the sanctified skies, which are one.
They touch fluidity fleetingly,
And splash goes my mind
In a split second of time.
I'm revealed a new energy thing
That keeps moving with its others
Of like motion till dusk.
Slowing like melatonin,
We fade within the brief,
Shadowy thoughtlessness of what was.
If I tried, then got no response,
Alibis they shared
I left in the wind.
Yesterday's faded memories—
They hear my inner voice.
And only now,
I listen for an echo
Of their new language
From miles where now I sense nothing
But the opposite,
They left like the wind
Before me.
You can only touch
What your senses can't reveal,
Because only under the surface
Is where I am real.
My life is parallel to yours.
You'll find out when you open doors,

Lead your imagination
To the garden of your mind,
And you'll stop denying
What it is you need to find.

Pie in the Window

Grandpa's smokin' a pipe, rockin' on the front porch in his usual chair.
Ma's hangin' clothes on the line while my sisters are braiding each other's hair.
I'm sneakin' around the corner of the house like I was some undercover spy,
Seein' if I can snatch me a piece of Ma's homemade apple pie.
I reckon no one will know, 'cause they're all so preoccupied.
Besides, I'd be foolish to let this chance slide by.
I don't want the whole pie, just a piece or two.
Oops, gotta watch it now; here comes that nosy neighbor, Sue,
Who has a laugh like a witch, but all she really is is a busybody,
Always watchin' for a chance to snitch on me.
So I believe I'll make a switch and go around the other way.
O Lord, forgive me for what I'm about to do today.
Ya know, Lord, I just wanna sliver or two.
I have to be inconspicuous around Ma,
Or she'll have me doing more than I want to.
And if Dad ever found out, he'd have my behind,
But he's too busy in the cellar makin' homemade wine.
I'm feeling nervous, and everything is all set.
But I still don't feel quite right yet.
So I looked up to the sky of blue and thought over my plan.
Just before I reached out with my guilty hand,
I stared back at how I felt in my heart.
I suppose the preacher woulda said I soon got smart.
So I let out a sigh, deciding to do what Ma wanted me to all along.
I began to feel better; I began to feel calm.
So I watered the garden, pulled some weeds;
I even fed that silly, lazy cat.
No one ever knew what I went through, and I guess I'll just keep it at that,
'Cause some things are better left unsaid—especially if you're to miss dessert,
Being sent straight to bed.

To steal and to lie over a piece of warm, tasty pie is not worth it.
Now it is easy for me to admit:
To think it through, you cannot afford to ignore.
So I'm gonna do me right just like I was told before.

Bare Bones

The bell rings; the candle burns.
The apparition touches gently
In a dark room—
No one there but the moon
Shining through.
That feels like so long ago
But may be just now—
A moment, a soul.
Autumn leaves whisper
In the cool evening breeze
That hears its own
Movement weary wave.
Silent roars don't forget
The doors unlocked.
Only unseen things
Fill the heart tonight.
Anywhere can be nowhere
Without a friend.
I dressed up for nothing;
My hat is my *crown*.
Isn't that something,
Even when no one's around?
Stillness won't be without notice
Tonight,
But what about the darkness
So bright?
You recall when we were everywhere—
We didn't budge an inch that night.

He Was Here

Where I go
Is where I live;
You can't come.
Another twilight
In my mind—
Time is done.

Intertwined,
Caught wandering,
As it was meant—
Dumbfounded
By the moment.

I know no more;
Time erased me.
All that I ever was
Is all I'll never be.

You who try so hard
Will never see:
Without eyes closed,
All that went
Was unknown by the moment.

What Love?

What love is there to find,
To melt my heart, to ease my mind?
What love is there to give,
To have, to hold, that will make me live?
What love is there for me to love,
To protect with grace that's from above?
What love could there be?
Who will just love, love me for me?
What love will last a lifetime—
The loyalty to be committed and be only mine?
What love have I now?
What does it disapprove? What does it allow?
What love have we here
That'll be enough to drive away the fear?
What love can change with the seasons,
That won't live in what-ifs or try to find reasons?
What love can I hope for, can I trust
When the fire is flickering and
The ashes are covered by dust?
When I'm gone and here no more,
Will I wake with you on another shore?
What love, what love is this?

Amanuensis

You wrote before you were born
And continue after each and every birth.
Your words are the words
Of the power of your birth
And everyone's birth.
You are always pregnant with
The meanings
Only they will reveal.
And for this, you will be used
By the meaning of the entire
Universe that flows through
Your mind and hand, which are one.
Your words are filled with
The sparks of the awakenings
That only souls that are
Present, open, and truly listening
Can gather.
Why they were written,
No matter how many births
They have or will experience—
You are the birth winter of many,
And the universe is your eternal inkwell.
And as you dip your mind
Into it as a quill.
Your brain will be guided
Only when you are ready.

The Many Are One

Falling
Spirit of light,
The one is
Hitting the mark;
The two are one.

I am sure
Life is a circle
To the point
Between the lines—
The place is you.

Slowly turning
In the eye of the needle
From so far away
Than I've ever been—
The soul searches itself.

Living on the edge of a dream,
Nothing is lost.
When the road meets you,
The love of your life—
It's never too late.

Silence is calling:
Set yourself free.
What love
Is falling for you?
Dwell upon the well and see.

Once,
A boy's redemption
Answered.
They are you;
This is why.

No one else will
When love is gone.
You are your teacher—
Paradigm,
Another way.

Stand your ground.
Love is always worth the risk—
None greater,
The one is
Frozen in time.

The prayer
Resting—
Forget me not.
Don't deny what's inside
In the presence of contrast.

The eternal stare
Will no longer break
The unconventional vision.
Judge yourself—
Not so fast.

One rose—
A survivor's touch,
A new language,
Secrets
God tells.

Two hands—
I'll learn;
I'll get it right.
The way is near,
Dusk in time.

Thoughts into Words

To your higher self:
If you are the master key,
Give thanks
In a world others created.
Now close them both;
Then step out on the edge with me,
Eye to loving eye,
Where nothing becomes everything.
Staring in the mirror,
Discover how much you find
The moment you caught yourself,
When you don't fall for all you can gain
But you reflected back to you,
Looking patiently within.
Some will stand; others will pray
To learn what is unexplainable.
Some will crack up; some will blow away—
Is more than chances can give.
The very blueprint of the inner universe—
It's up to the power of meaning.
You can follow the rhythm on the map.
So the dimensions you ponder are deeper—
Life gave it to you—
Than the oceans of drops that flow
Across the orbit of your soul,
Together instantly.
You remembered before the story was over,
When you stop and begin to turn
Their thoughts into words,
Into the valleys of life—what it takes.
Others will learn
To get near the lights,

Reflecting your inner, new way
As you climb,
Your heart to your mind,
Thinking gently about all that connects.

Two Hands

Both hands reach out
From two people.
This man, this woman,
Reaching slowly with their fingertips,
Touching one another's faces,
Feeling warm skin:
Cheeks, lips, and chin.
Sensations flow to their minds
Of emotions creating images inside,
Put together by the sound
Of breath that comes out
And goes back in again.
Two sightless people find life
And drink of its essence,
Seeing with one quiet moment
On a windy Sunday afternoon
At someone's home alone.
What we had become
Has led us to this catching,
Perfect creation
That gives a taste of bliss.
What we were before
Will never be again.
Everything moves and changes,
Because there is no end.
I face the facts
Of the face I'll never see
With my outer eyes,
But I will see
Between the dark and the light
With the feeling I feel
When I touch the sensations bright

That are there and real.
No more wandering in the dark,
No more fear in the heart—
Only movement from impulse.
I'm drawn to what creates life,
Movement touching
Between the day and the night—
What two hands can do
Sees another way for the few
Who have been given new eyes to see
That touch only what is true.

Let It Rain

The conscience
Left in suspense
By the shrinking evidence
Of innocence
When should I go
Where could I hide
For one human soul
Too much inside

The dove is crying
The wind is still.
Time is ticking away
On my windowsill.
Doors unlocked.
Ground damp wet.
From the rain that came
After sunset

There's too much of
Everything
That there can possibly be
Does love stand a chance
In a death defying society

The deacon was drinking
In a nook
Off beside the library
Reading a book
He mumbles to himself
That he remembered
Every line
But knows

Even what grows
Soon will wither on the vine

I've been on both sides
One is crumbling
The other hides

I'm welcome by both
But still in the heart
Of my will

I don't fit in these clothes
So I walk the fence
That makes no sense
To all the onlookers
Who carry on in their emptiness
I'll continue
With me, myself, and I
The conscience
Scrying roots of suspense
By the expanding evidence
To the bias

Where I humbly reveal
The reality no one can conceal
Enough freedom within
Which is given
To those who desire to know
No one
Really has that far to go.

In Memory

Heaven took someone dear
Close to us
Now all we think about
Is how he really was
Like St. Peter and St. Paul
He was an inspiration to us all
A friend to the lonely
A brother that stuck closer
Than you and me
He was a natural
Like we ought to be
A warrior
Like an angel always near
He taught us courage in battle
How to conquer fear
Sovereign circumstances no one
Could control
Took him many times
Around the mountain
Awaiting the salvation of his soul
Morning after morning
We remember your face
Bright and warm
You must've had the light
The day you were born
Everyone's days are numbered
Like the hairs on our heads
None of us are ever sure
If tomorrow we'll awake
From our beds
So many times your day
Seemed near

You never wavered in faith
But always persevered
Now no more waiting
Or painful battles too
Just a constant, peaceful dawn
Calmly shining over you
As you sing your song
Lead me on
There's a thin line
Between life and death
We come to realize
Since you left
What you taught us we can't forget
It's like you're here
But we're not ready yet
When we think of him
He remembers us
But all our thoughts of him
Are how he really was
On the earth side temporal and frail
We often cry, we often fail
The glass is so very dim
But for you it's clear
'Cause you're *home now*
The likes of you are hard to find
Precious and rare
We know the glorious rewards
Are yours
Forever you will wear
You left suddenly
Like a warm breeze
That quietly leaves
The depths of this life's valleys
Yes, heaven took you, our beloved
We always miss and remember when
But we have true hope in seeing you
Again.

Marriage of the Heart

Old in soul
Young in heart
Married in spirit
Never apart
Where ever we are
Continue to live
Through one another's mind
One of a kind
You and I
We will be
As we always were
A day at a time
Safe'n'secure
You are mine
I am yours
It's the deeper
The sweeter
The more peaceful and content
It's not in the showy
Or in all the money you spend
No need for happy anniversary cards
As nice'n'as sweet as they are
For the married of the heart
These things
Always come with love
Surprising unexpectedly
As naturally life gives with its variety
People that see us
Talk like we were
Meant to be
So why would we
Jeopardize it with something

That would cause it to be temporary
With all the other things
That don't last too
The flowers, the hours
Of work that could
Never save us too
But only marriage of the heart
Will continually make us new
Where there's no tuxedos, no prayers
Or church isle to walk
No, we don't mind let them all talk
'Cause we're secure, happy, and content
Right where we are
Lovingly resting in each other's heart.

Bury Me without the Key

Arrest me from myself
Take me away
So I can be someone else
Lock me up
Throw away the key
Let my shadow go
So I can finally be
I'm seeing Houdini
Inside this cell of signs
He's raising the pin
As I'm no longer
Doing time
I'm released
The moment
You slam the door
I saw this all coming
I'm sure someone else
Will do it too
Just like I've done before
There's no reason or sense
To ever stay the same
'Cause the anger and the madness
Within the stranger and his sadness
Only begins
When the idle one
Has too much time to spend
In the aimlessness of a
False freedom
That can never deliver.
Brush away what you see
True freedom comes
When you're lock'd up

Without a key
That only your mind
Knows how to turn
And set you free
When you let rock bottom
Create a reality
Of your own
You'll find out
What no one else
Has never known
You can't make
Anything happen
Because
It's already happening
You are
What's happening.
Wander in your dreams
Crawl in your streams
Feel the magic
In all the scenes
Follow that breath
Until you claw your way
Right on out of your
Own muddy grave
That has become
The very love
Within that saves you
From yourself
Only you
And nobody else.
Bury me without the key
And I'll be free.

Not Just Another Fish

Before my daddy died
He had one last wish
That I would go down
And catch 'em a big ol' fish
Bring it on home
Clean out all its bones
Fry it up and serve it to 'em
In his old supper dish

So I left home early next morn
With my pole in one hand
And bait in the other
I was as quiet as a mouse
So I wouldn't wake my little brother
Dream'n about myself
Listen'n to my mind talk
Birds were chirp'n
Sun was com'n up
As I was walk'n down the walk
Proud to be a fisherman
Proud to be a boy
Proud of the opportunity
To bring somebody some joy
By the time I got to the pond
It was 6:30 on the nose
I wore my usual fish'n attire
Look'd like Huck Finn's clothes
From the top of my head
Down to my dirty toes
I sat down by the edge of the water
Threw the line out as far as she could go
Then I sat back and watched

That wiggly little worm
Put on quite a show
Man oh man, he sure did show off
The ripples in the calm water
Made me laugh
As I tried to hold back
An early morn'n cough
So I wouldn't scare off any fish
Dream'n and scheme'n
How I'd catch Pap a big old daddy catfish

First fish nibbled enough to tease
Had a third my bait gone
So I brought 'em in
And put on another one
He was long and shiny
Just like the skies above
I was doin' this fish'n
'Cause my pappy
Know I was happy
Doin' something I really love'd

All of a sudden my pole
Practically jerked right out of my hand
Felt like Moby Dick pull'n
On the other end
It was the daddy all right
Taken my line
For a wild ride
So I play'd with 'em
Just for fun
And after a minute or two
I thought that catch'n
Time was due
My forehead damp
My fists clamped

On that pole
For dear life
I kick'd out of my bag
With my foot
That shiny, silver cutt'n knife
I was reel'n slow
As he got closer
Jump'n out of the water
Six foot high
He jumped so high
Look'd like a bird in the sky
So I let 'em fly
He squirmed and he pulled
And by then I reach'd out to grab 'em
He was a twenty-pounder for sure
His eyes a wink'n
And gasp'n all over
Its wet, slick form

Then I threw 'em in the pale
And I shouted, "I got the meal!"
In the wind that blew
From the oncoming storm

On the way home
My heart was roar'n
It was pour'n
And I was soaked
Running in through the back door
Thinkin that Pop had already woke
But he wasn't there
As water dripped off my hair
I look'd in despair
For my Pop had passed away
Before I could make 'em
The fish I caught today …

But just then, a foghorn blew
Pop walk'd in with pole in hand
And said, "Hey, sleepyhead,
You gonna sleep the day away?"
Half awake, I barely thought to myself
It all seemed so real
I thought again how great it feels
To be together again.
Both of us walk'n down
Together to the docks
Sitting there in the sunshine
On those old, eternal quarry rocks.

What Was After All

The thread broke
the last leaf I did see
fell on November thirteen
now laying quietly
without a sound
dark was the sky
so was the ground
no wake, no funeral
no more harvest
celebration
colors of death's hope
all gone
now the cold
bites the air
into the inevitable
to come along
soon buried
now dried up
slowly crumbling on.

Silence Is Calling

Memory still the same
Eyes closed in heaviness
We are young again
Stones walk upon
Dusk as a new world
Old murmur
Leaving red in the west
So far away now
Peaking she does
My loves loving sighs
I can hear but not see myself
Silence hides the dark brim
Before we feed each other
All the stars falling
Hide-and-seek it's all a game
What did she mean
Of never mind
I travel upon a path
And also in another era
Somehow unknown to anyone I was
Unlike Northern Ohio
As you draw nigh
Night kisses the light good-bye
My flesh and some crumble
Up the street in steam
Flickering candles lit
Before we come together
I've got a cloud to catch
All around a dreamless twilight
Everywhere I could be
My name is called
Edges of what is

Lingers throughout our time
We came back another way
A horse drives us with the top down
Hope for the escaping stillness
Somewhere
Unlike I do now here today.

More than Dirt

You're more than halfway home
If you got the guts to look out over
The infinite Grand Canyon

Many have, some want to and
There are those who don't have
The courage to think about it, yet

It's a desire given, not earned
To go home is where all you have learned
Is the way we all eventually let go
Of all that has held us back
Now that you've been before
You came after you were born

That sacred place where spirits always know
That one life at a time is all about
The one you're standing in right now

When your breath reaches the edge
Eyes so wide when you stay still so close
To your home, your heartbeat, you realize for sure
You know forever more that you are more
Than dirt, much more

Come on let's take a little walk on home
I want to take you to a higher place
Don't ask where it is, just follow me
Now count the drops when it lightly rains
Because everything between you and I
We live in different worlds for now
But one day the same

It's right here where we are
To go there while you're here
All you have to do is remember
It's where you live and breathe
Home is not home unless you're there
As the raindrops slowly halted to a stop
We began to reflect each other on each one
I said, "Watch out. Here comes the sun."

**It dawned on us as we noticed we were always home
Dripping mirrors to each other in an endless sea
On our little walk home.**

One Rose

You are my food
You are my drink
You are my thoughts
That I think

You are my feelings
That I know are real
You are the feelings that I feel
When nothing else will

You are the true love
I've waited for
The love I love
And completely adore

You are the one rose
Kissing lightly upon my cheek
You are the one I chose
I will keep.

A Moment of Intent

Another face
I'll never see again
In the crowds
Floating by
Like shadows in the clouds
Silvery linings
Upon the time
As I strolled downtown
Horse carriage
Clopping along
On Saturday no marriage
To bring tears
Or a song
Sirens, parades, create charades
Of all kinds
Open up your windows
As you draw down
The blinds
Feeling scents
Autumn's crumbling rhyme
When comes she does
Cleavage pronouncements
In the leafy streets
Angelic eyes
Go before cuteness
All around the corners
Falling sands
Touching shoreline
Reaching out to
The delicate one you choose—single
Men secretly gawking who
Feel they have

No one to lose
I notice fall's attire
Like my love she does
Change my desire
The train whistle blows
As it lightly rains
By the lake of
Do you remember when
For in a distant place
A time like this
Is never that far away
From bliss
My nearest heaven
There's another antique shop
Displaying what I've been
Seeing, walking around me
All day long
Through burnt, orange brick walls
The years come to me
Staring into the beyond
Where ever it may end up
I'm sure as I get there
I'll recall my now
But it's gone again
A moment of intent
Whisperings
Through a laying dog's raised ears
To be a part
I'm simply glad to be
Where all those
I never met
But peacefully
Blindly I did see
Like resurrected statues
We all move about

Unknowingly till we gasp
We remember everything
All over again
In a new way.

Let the Eye Follow Itself

Crushed in schmaltz
Crumpled leaves
My nephew dead or alive
Sitting before me eye to eye
With the spirit board
Remained a tight cord
By my side briefly
I have no temperament
For such nonsense as that
Who cannot receive from my defense
That knows no true whereabouts
Or hangout for the time to adore
I shall take my leave
As so did he and be no more
I am humbled by the gracious
Who live beyond the sacred door
Open to me not a word
But could fill volumes
In my being never absurd
Yes, I'd rather walk alone
Than to be the truly false listener
Of those who don't care
In hopes that in my disgust
I will make sure that which
Is tossed in the dust
Here no more again
For every time when around the world
Is the end
But I think I shall not catch
A greater song sent
As when I hear the melody of sunset
As you will
Peace be still.

I'm Not You

Knowing yourself
Is worth more than
You'll ever know.
You've trapped yourself
Inside the words
you say
Obviously it's a place
You cannot get away
So go ahead
Put another block
Upon your wall
See how much shorter
You can make it
For a lesser fall
Your thoughts
They swarm around you
Like bees
To protect you from
The things
You really need
To set yourself free
You have to perceive
Have faith you say
But you know
that's all
Just make-believe.
So pretend
till the end
What you'll find
And you'll understand
It's more than a state of mind.
Blame is put on me

For the things
You do yourself
Then you tell me
To go get some help
I listen to you
Till I cannot think
Insanity is always
On the brink.
You never really learned
That self-praise stinks
Every time
You gaze in the mirror
You give yourself another wink.

House of Sorrow

Lights all out
Doors locked
The leather belt
Was swift and hot
Burning and stinging me
Every shot
Pain pours like rain
Exploding down my spine
Through my brain
Till every nerve in my mind
Went totally blind
From the strain
But I still love you
Because a little boy
Doesn't know what to do
But this little boy
Grew up angry inside
Because of the times
He died and died and died
Bitter little boy
Falls asleep in the rain
Wakes up slow
Wipes away the snow
Off his mane
Only to find
He's got nothing but pain
To live for
His night is like light
Now and forever more
But I still love you
He says
He knows not

What is true
Every unkind face
Is a trap to him
Or a slap to him
When he walks out his
Door
Or goes through a store
All I know,
You're all I have today
If there's tomorrow
The home I grew up in
House of sorrow
So familiar with grief
The distraction will always
Come
From being so numb
For so long
Everything that looks so good
Feels so wrong
Deep, deep inside
Where I can't hide
All the times
I died and died and died.

Make Your Stand

Making your stand
the hard way
has spelled out the direction
while contemplating the moments
of a possible life.
Experiences in action
where there's always
something new
as you choose to
reach within knowing
what others only dream
to believe.
My friends
from the old world
dare me not
to spare
the time so rare
with those who don't care.
Measure your own steps
for all of us are
always learning
simple and true.
Together we'll understand and achieve
the fulfillment
beyond our own power
of gifts and talents.
Re-enforce the magic
of all that is possible
for our fates
do not rest in the
hands of a few.
Because our dreams

do not challenge what
seems beyond the stars
that extend above the
heights within us.
So gallantly we take
charge of our own
so others will do
in every golden chance.
That we were discerning
the greatest of all
reaching within to make your stand.

Need to Be Needed

I dreamt about you dreaming
Is this a double life
Or is it just the night
Sincerely I agree
We know more than we realize
But none can help
The wounded like the wounded
If we have courage
To love those who don't
Really like us
Because sometimes bad things happen
For good reasons
Either way only a fool
Tries to destroy
Evil with hatred and bloodshed.
So could it be that the mouth is
The door to the heart
If the eye is the window to the soul
If change is the most reliable resource
The world has ever known
Than it is true
That it is hard to tell the truth
When you're lying is it not
But the sun shines again
Only when we help each other
In our needs.
This is why we need to need
So we can see the light again.
For my angels watch over you
Like yours do me
We're all connected

Because of what will surely be.
Think well of one another all day long
Then you will know what it means
To make each other strong.

Serenity Significance

Retiree looks back
Thirty years pass
Like a moment
In a flash
From an invisible
Camera
No one can see

There's a young
Child
Running wild
In these desperate
Worldly streets
Abandon from home

Relationships
Leave many tips
In your mind
On paper slips
Where ups and downs
Rights and wrongs
Don't do a thing
For you or me

Someone led Johnny
Down a dead-end road
Now he's gazing through
Steel bars
Wondering what went wrong
He can't even picture
What could possibly be

Is there significance in a home
Does it whisper on the phone
Or have flesh and bone
Everyone I ask
Seems to know
Where and how to find
This lonely peace

There's a city man
A country woman
Pretending like they were taught
To capture a certain destiny
But their act is just a fact

The preacher needs a teacher
The newsman doesn't understand
Philosophies run dead on
Straight into oblivion
Where all the answers
Don't connect
Giving too much for listeners
To expect
Everyone keeps on getting hungry

A boy without a father
Stares out at the stars above
Thinking about a fading
Memory of his father's love
Which he'll always long to see
As tears roll down his face
Wishing he were me

Two men argue over a woman
Neither one of them
Really know
She's trapped in the middle
Because she's got no place to go

Here comes a crippled girl
Staggers on two silver legs
Her house is warm
Where she was born
But wearing only rags

Rich man, poor man
A lot of times, don't understand
Without some kind of money
What they want isn't what
They really need
Everyone has inside them
A river that bleeds
Every now and then
Everyone has an opinion
A certain amount of sensitivity
That they are searching for

Painter dreams peering
At the mountaintops
Poet ponders sipping coffee
At the coffee shops
Factory worker joking
To help others make it through
Another day of monotony

Wounded heart of a man hurting
But everyone thinks he's crazy
In a world void of concern

Our heart of beauty gives us wisdom
To really know the difference
The courage to change
In our weakness and humanity
Grant us a lasting life
Filled with real serenity.

Falling

There is one small
Light-colored feather
Falling through the openness
And as it
Goes
And leaves a trail
Of itself to all those
Observing its freedom
To flow
With gentleness that
Hopes to find a home
Somewhere
Inside
The lightness may
Show itself
That there is no fear
In slowly falling
When you know
You're going home.

The Old Evil Eye

The man looks in the mirror
Says to himself within
I have no fear
Steps out into the night
He's ready to fight
His right hand
Clenched into a fist
Hard and tight
Down the road he goes
Till he vanishes out of sight
Gazing into the twilight
Alone in a starry sky sure
He hears the voices again
You're a failure
A blinking, winking evil eye
In a quiet, watery cry
Where he himself inside
Will not surrender and die
But will fight on from dusk till dawn
To get by
He fades once again
Into the welcoming wind
Where magic begins and ends
Thoughts twist and blend
Like a long-lost friend
He pulls out
Of the inside pockets
Of his soul
All the memories
That made him grow
Into what he is today
A man burnt, a man hurt

In a night fading away
Can't change the past
Tomorrow totally uncertain
Only tonight he has the right
To be whispering to himself
About all the times
He could not help
But had to stand alone
Now he's grown
Heart like a stone
Bitter to the bone
From all the mislead neglect
Others have sown upon him
He knows his twin
Is favored to win within
But he doesn't care anymore
Not friendly fire
He's worried about
It's the meaning behind the war
Like an unknown soldier
Who floats passed his grave
He sees others crying
So in vain
Now he's finally numb
To the pain
That used to haunt him
Again and again
The battle is over
The walk of the narrow night
Is through
The single dance
Of tenderness
Has forever forgotten
The likes of him too
Right smack dab into
The middle of all he held true

Known unknown soldiers
Visited lonesome prisoners
Sung with unsung heroes
Planted seeds where no one goes
Leaving a world a place
Where others say
He will be safe
All the rest of his days.

Was There

There was
A fire, a night, marshmallows
The moon and you
I didn't have a chance.
Everything was in
The history books before
We got there.
All we ever wanted
In our lives
Was there
In a perpetual moment
Us two.
The spirit
Was at its height
Everything was right
That clear emotion
Of love
In a scene
Will always be alive
An imprint in time
Means something
No one can deny.
In the laughter—complete
Reception
Nature happily gathers
In the only direction
Within
On a perfect
Autumn flight
With you.

Bound by What's Up

I picked somebody's brain apart
Saw their thoughts in my heart
When I was asleep
By the time I asked my brother
Where he was
He answered, "Right here"
My clock started to beep
Into your eyes
I went for another view
Slowly I suddenly realized
My feelings were being stirred
In someone's homemade stew
Everywhere I turned
I remembered what someone else
Said they haven't learned
By myself without anyone's help
Floating through a cracked door
Came out of a mirror
From the bride's room above the floor
The ceiling fan was going round
She left like a puff of smoke
For I am sunken in the heavenly
Earthbound world by a hanging rope.
There's a cemetery in every heart
We go back there every time
As we listen
We take part in what happened
Because we know no matter
How long ago there's no end
To really what was
We go back to the movements
The cause which is synonymous and

Pay our respects
To what changed and rearranged us
In the foggy mist
There we were covered in dust
Reaching up way back
For that invisible hand
To take ours to help us
Through the hours that will last
As long as timelessness exists
We have to come back
To the room where the cemetery
Lays before us all, calling us to gather
Making our light bright with what's right
Into the morning I will walk.
Your rays hitting me like tickling feathers
In the dewy breeze
You were always with me and always will be.
Right before me she sheds her past
Everything I like reveals dreams never die
I saw the haunted
In the middle of the night
I knew something was happening
The moment you were born
As the air split the space, the light burst open wide
The subtleties of the seas began to lead me outside
Pioneers from the front to the rear say,
"Everybody's following something within"
I'm transfixed on my fire from the sun
Who leads me with love
To my one again
For the only way out
Is in.

I Will Awake

Like autumn
leaves I must
leave
but I will become
unlike before
because you will see
I will be
so much more
the day will break
light will dawn
I will awake
and sing a new
song
that only trees
can give birth to
when the green of green
will be brand new
as I reach for the
heavens again that shine,
darken and blow with wind
I will proudly decay in
color and whisper
as I fall and gently leave
become so much more
as a mighty tree.

For Every Poet

She looked back
Somewhere in time
Hoping to find what she
Left behind
In a poet
Thought about them all
With admired affection
Everyone knows rejection
Has learned to fall
Living outside always looking in
The amazement of it all
Drinking every drop
Till every sip in your heart is dry
Knowing full well
That every star will one day die
From that inner drive
Wonderful strangeness
Whispers
We are all
Self-made entities
Of our own choosing
Begins in
The mind's eye to see
Consciously we seek
The beauty of death
In life
The goal of the ages
For many to be
You gotta write
Tired feet
See once again
Every road bends

Eventually
Exposing fibers of spirit
No room to split hairs
The naked truth
Can destroy or give birth
To all the revelation of nightmares
Shining mirrors
The world to come
Everyone
No tricks, games, gimmicks
The light is not the sun
But you—the one in the one
Who climbs that
Steep hill
Like the love in her heart true
In the alley
Realizing the lust—he now embraces
Leaving him in the dew
Beyond what is real
The flash of the
Quill
O sprite feather died
Let your experiences be your guide
Makes quality by the strength
Of the will
Who remains when all has gone
Give more than to receive
Live more than to believe
Upon every word of every line
If for only one in mankind
You're a bridge a galaxy
Emptiness between you and the poet
That be
Who lives, dies by the stroke of the pen
Sees through women and men
Capturing innocence

Of children on a playground
To every poet
For every poet
Will come back again.

To Fall Prey

Love me, but don't love me too much
You may fall prey to my touch
Love me, but don't give in all the way
You may fall prey to wanting me every day
Love me, but don't love me like it's the last day of your life
You may fall prey to becoming my wife
Oh, just love me for love's sake
Let's see how much love we can make
Just don't make love like there's no tomorrow
For you may fall prey to that piercing sorrow
Just love me, Let yourself just rain and drip all over me
So we both can be the love
To lift each other's life far above today
While other's fall prey in their own way.

In the Presence of Contrast

Who can ignite the fire
Who needs a little push
Will I learn by my desire
Standing before the burning bush?

I've repressed and forgotten
Every wrong moment of the past
Now I stand the test of time
In the presence of contrast.

Where is your son tonight
Who needs a little shove
Will he entertain the mysteries
Or stand before the burning love?

I have longed in the journey
Love and faith wait in the wing
Never ever impatient
To give what I must bring.

Let me know where to go
Let me be in the voice
As the night moves slowly
Into the moment of one's choice.

When the wind is quiet
And the mountains are still
Let me feel your power
Flood every pore of my will.

Then I stand before the pain
Then I'll kneel before the naked
And reveal without a word
In the spirit of what was said.

The light that lights up the night
That makes one's choice very clear
Let the one that dares to know
Have ears to really hear.

Within All of Me

Thick atmosphere
Tumbling in my bed
Laying inside the bubble
Like waters adrift
A revelation
To my individuality
I'm always
Somewhere else as well
The transcendence
Draws nets
Only by the immense
Reflection that sends
Answering
My own questions
It's faint
When gazing myself
In mirror
Seeing my others
Lives that dwelt
Among the ones
I am.

Where We Are Lead Now

Where we are lead
By who knows who
Giving us time
To be in the now
Of the past ahead
Hopefully in the arms of
Sun rays that show
That sudden flash will
Above our minds below
The eyes of clarity
We are all
Filling the role
With that
Light of thought
Unseen will echo
Castle of the soul
Remind us what resembles
We will know
Once alive within
These temples
Now are as ghosts
Concealed
Will be
Everything
Gone into the unknown
At once
No flesh 'n' bone
We're released
When our time
Is behind
Needs will cease
We

All
The conscience
Left, in suspense
By shrinking evidence
Wandering innocence
Forever
In us
Fading as the mist.

No One Ever Told You

The ground you stand on
Are the shoes
That helped you walk there
You have not truly loved
Until you have loved the unlovable
For life feels short
Only to those who don't know
We say the most
When we don't say a thing
In silence we bare the truth
Of who and what we are
To ourselves and one another
In the perfect spirit of timing
Saying I'm sorry
Doesn't change a thing
Smoothed over are the moments
Till you do it again
But my inner
Tells my outer
To hesitate before I say
Let them go their own way
To begin
So it is an internal fact
The most reliable source
Humanity has in its grasp
Is 'Change'
And nothing else
For without this understanding
Her heart
Like the softness of a rose
Plunged it in the thorn
She bled all over

The one she took within
After believing
Now her scar
Is on the lips
Of another heart
As the previous red stain
Goes free
For some must pass
In order for a petal
To become
Truly one
Again.

Unconventional Vision

Don't try to make sense
When there's no time to waste
I saw your curls cover your breasts
Like the birds who flock
Over the trees
Everyone is always surprised
When no one lives and no one dies
Don't forget the coins you tossed
Or the wishes you dream't at dusk
Everyone wonders every now and then
But don't try and understand
Spread your arms like they are wings
And cover all her heart
Till you love and sleep in for a while
Forget about what was
To live in the feel of the afterglow
Hand me my magnifier and push my pen
Read the letters no one writes or sends
Keep quiet, let the train say what the night
Has long been overdue
Give me a look that's all I need
Come a little closer
My sleepy-eyed unconventional vision
From an era when hats
Were worn like crowns
Ladies and gentlemen
So watchful
Invisibly telling the moments
That were coming for tomorrow
If I fade before you finish

Let the pipe drop on the wood
That can't be burnt
For we can settle the score
Yet another day.

No Interruptions

A radio
Sings with no ads
Just help, love
And all that jazz

Give me that
Which is up at
I'll go if you want
Treasuring the beat pizazz

I love it
When you're near
While waves of silence
Take us to another new
Like no one else has

Darkness is subtle and sure
Vibes right where we dream
It's real stereo from chrome
A $1.73 for a gallon of gazz
No interruptions, no commercials
Just sweet melody for me and my baby.

Wandering Away, Dream Relief

When I first
Learned the golden rule
A boy in a Catholic school
Lost in safety town
With the rest of the
Dead-end kids
In the middle
At grade one
In between two arguing nuns
As the class
Played and had fun
Altar boys light the candles
With a wink or grin for a sign
The Father stumbles up to the altar
A bit too much blood
They call wine

I daydreamed
So easily it seemed
Watching snow
Outside the classroom window
I was not the nun's favorite
Because I did not act like a pet
Many things back then I did forget
But the things I hadn't
Like all the world and its scenes
All the time I wandered
In my daydreams

They took me where
Books would not dare
It made me realize

About a special place
That drew me there
Till I got a brand-new taste
Of what it all really means
To journey through a school day
Floating and escaping within my thoughts

There's really much more
To all of this
But I don't believe
That there possibly is
Enough paper in the world
To explain the bliss
Of what it all really means
To be a boy
Captivated by his dreams

I look forward earnestly to see you
I'm teaching myself
So we can start all over again
To walk with you in the newness of day
When everything is different
We are not the same

I listen to your heart
Beating close to mine
I watched you play in the fields
Then quenching your thirst with life's new wine
You kissed my eyes so gently
As you wandered into invisibleness
I thought of you
Till it took me where you were
In the distance

To live in light that will never go out
I tell you the waters around here
Flow and shimmer
Your countenance so fair and true
So close to me I walked right through you
You whispered we must be a traveling
So I held your hand as we got closer
To that place

This little girl ran right up to me
She said—Hey, Daddy, with a smile,
You're so funny
Her arms full of love, full of dreams
As she laughed by the clear, crystal streams
My life is so full now
Because of you
It's joyful so radiant and true

Still don't really know
If it could happen or not
Cause what I was taught by others
It takes more than love to be
One for a lifetime
But with you, I'm not afraid
To be a fool and try
When all I have left is time

Maybe, we'll have that chance
In the months ahead
Where we breathe together
In a place we can call our own forever.

Love Is Always Worth the Risk

Alone inside the world
You and I create
With creation that surrounds us
Our love and growth
That will not hesitate
Alone at last with you
And the pure, blue naked sky
The river too sparkles like glass
When I gaze in your eye
I'm somebody, I'm fulfilled
I'm drenched in life beyond my will
Your presence gives me a place
I've never known before
Your heart, your face
Opens every door
Every season is ours
To be raised into newness of love
We have every emotion and reason
To dream the dreams
Only eternal lovers think of
Never will the heart and its beauty '
Be forsaken as mine
For in every sacred moment
It's always divine
I will either live loving you or die trying to
For some now must love
For tomorrow may never come.

Flesh and Blood

My flesh and blood
You got that way by my love
Don't know where
Or when, how or why it happened.

Took a little bit of faith
Mixed in a bottle
Of messages I couldn't ignore
Like light years away
I hardly see you anymore.

But you are my flesh and blood
I know it's hard to understand
When love is the only one
Unseen hand.

Now the world today
Is lost in its heart
Rolling sideways
On a one way start
That seems to have no end
Even though I see you both
In the faces and the places I've been.

You are my heart and joy
You got that way
One day
You don't know how or why
Sometimes I ask myself
Just who am I.

You take pieces of my soul
Like a puzzle to fit
In time that flies by
That won't ever quit
Mixing my memories
With pictures
I'll never ignore
I've sacrificed myself
So no one will know me
Anymore.

The Eternal Stare

I am a soul
That cannot be defined
By man or his religion
I have not
So fallen as quickly
As by bullet, arrow, wind,
Earthquake or the mighty animal
As I have by
The humbleness
That came by
The gaze upon the eyes
Of the leaving, transitioning soul
Staring off into infinity
Like a dream playing the gentle music
Of what will never be again
I've never known
Anyone truly ready
For it comes without
Regard
For ones holiest desire
To remain as one is now
Keep your vigil
After day break
Keep it in the silence
Of the night
Know yourself to be
Known only
Most importantly by
The moments that dwell within
Humble and true with light
No matter how small or bright

With peace, good intentions
Always near
For the eyes that will open
To the eternal stare.

Open Message

Without a prayer
She bit my tongue
To help me see where
I bleed
Is the message
From the messenger
Who always tells you in secret
That you know words
Are only for those who can feel
Without trying
The energies of the thoughts
That are born and live in the air.
Down below the mind
For lifetimes of hurt will
Suddenly understand and discern
What only a few can realize
When everything can automatically
Rewind itself until there's
A perfect blank mind again
To fill up hopefully with
No blood in the mouth
But with words for all
To be healed with.
Now out of the well
Ready to go west—I
Snuck in the side
Of the bait room
But was never confirmed
For sure.
The wish lets the door
Close where it will — you have to trust
Your best instincts in spite

Of all negativity
Go the direction that opens up to you
Like the wind moving away
From where you stand
Safer in the city alone
Than in the country on your own
When you are slowed down or stopped
No matter how long it takes
The twenty-four-hour news is never done
We haven't even yet begun.
Your shadow was never cross
While sleepless eyes look tired and lost
Sitting in your office
Cold and hard like a vault
Where you decide others destiny by fault
With copy machine, computer key punch
Slowly give way to headache after headache
No time to unwind or break
Drained before the day even starts.
Haven't got a prayer
Hear the hum of gossip
Slowly prepare
Act like there's no care
About all the silence
That suddenly will fill the room.
Walk in
Just a ghost now
A figment of the imagination
The stage is set, the lights are on
The thoughts and feeling are flying
Walking by
Like nothing's wrong.
The intuitive viewer now seeks
To try to patch up the leaks
Smooth over what's been said
Now for weeks.

The violins begin to play
As the cold snow slowly melts and
Fades away
Lost for the first time
On what exactly to say
Daydream about the misery
When you lost me
You crushed me down to earth soul
The memories that flashed by
So fast are now buried
Like graves in a row.

In the Living Heart of One Open Eye

If beauty and truth
Are in the eye
Of the beholder
Than ugliness and lies
Are too
If the two become
One
From the sight within
How much more the love
Could there be won
When open
To bring opposites together
As life like
You and I
Perhaps
There we would all see
Aright
Without judgment
On each other
In the gray
Of wisdom's light.

Falling for You

As I edge my way
Along life's tight wire
Nothing to say as I fall prey
Wounded by friendly fire
In the heat of the night
The sniper wore a shield
Carrying a long, silver knife—but
He pulled out his gun
And shot me just the same
Because I was on the run
And he needed someone to blame
Now I'm in this bed
With my face toward the sun
In an unending dream
Watching all I had done
10,000 white birds
That look like doves
Swirl around my bed
Leading me up the stairway
Through the clouds in my head
To a place I've never been before
Time and space are closing in
Tunneling me to the door
That's slightly ajar
With lights shooting out
All I feel is peace and warmth
And nothing to doubt
I know who I am
But not where I'm going
On my way to somewhere
I'm ready to go – taking a short cut
And taking it nice and slow

It's definitely a place
Where everyone recalls my face
But can't remember my name
I guess this is why
I never go back
The same way I came
As I fall
Fall once again for you.

All Our Outlets

Letting go
Is always left for me
I can taste it
Others can't budge
Don't really need to know much
With every breath
We all dare
To do each other
One possibly last favor
By the dripping dusk
That swims through
Giving invisibly
Your holy contemplations freely
In the instant you entered
The pouring sensation
Devouring the missing ones
Again no one
Boasts or gloats
By the loyal stripes we survive
Under a waving, waning moon
In the indigo eyes we blend
For now I have
No faith in yesterday
I raised my own life
Bringing blankets for
The lonely bare trees
For every receiver of the
Art will return
Wood, hay, stubble
Will burn
Flower in brick pots
Will hug and tug together

Reminding me as I
Stroll by
The power of loves
Staring glance
Suave, debonair nature's air
Breathing in residue
Of all places simultaneously
Nothing is ticking away
Tricked by the unmelting
That is not happening
We get the closest
To what is only with
Open heart, closed eyes
People try to fill a void
By doing those things
They say they enjoy
That most will take with themselves
To relive
Again.

West Park Street

Early each morning
He heard the phone ringing
Be up?
Gathered the gang
Bats, gloves, gum
Never forgot cut-ups
Run'n in the wind
Sweet laughter and sweat
Anger and competition
Made it worth more
Than a bet
Johnnie and I
End'd in cokes
Too tired to run
So ready to hide
Left the game
That never ends
No one ever wins
When you're all friends
it's laughter and camaraderie
Make'n fun of each other's built
Skinny or fat
No one could swing
A mean'r bat
Than Johnnie and I
In the mud, pouring rain
Scorching sunshine
We push'd the limits
One would leave
Everyone eventually quits
But no one ever really wins
In the game that never ends

Cause we're all just cut-up friends
Wanting nothin'
But have'n it all
Every kid big and small
Johnnie and I
End'n it in cokes
Till another summer morning
For another early phone ringing
Later, Johnnie
Later, Oz.

Lone Soldier

I'm in the body
That's dying
I'm in the spirit
That's crying
Through your walls
Doors and windows
I'm the one you hear
Calling
Whenever the wind
Blows
When you see
The sea roll
The sunshine glow
The moon bright
Where the river flows
I'm in your morning light
I'm in your colors of the
Rainbow
A lone soldier
Reaching out on the
Highest peak
I'm in the rain that falls
I'm in the eyes
Of a new born babe
About to speak
A lone soldier who always
Was and always will be
I'm the one you can sense
But cannot actually see
But for real it's me
In the corner of your eye
Right above your heart

I'm there gently
Touching your hair
When you're asleep in bed
I live for each
Moment new
More than I ever had
If I'm the one
You miss
Then I'll be the one
Who'll make you glad
Because I'm the one
You always wanted
But never had
But when the stars
Shine tonight
You won't see me
But you'll feel me
In the light
Giving you back all
What you lost in time
Those rare moments.

Every Direction by Twilight

We live in a psychic world
Where nothing's new
Everyone knows and shows you
Exactly what to do
Call today and find out
It's in the mind
No one's really blind
To what it's all about
No info is sacred anymore
Exposed secrets, you're trapped
Privacy slapped
Where you were before
Know your *own* destiny
The answer is for sure
It travels by energy
From the time you awake
Learn what you will see
On the road of life
If you need a job or a wife
By daybreak
Life and death is in the palm
The past and future
Is in the present cure
So just be calm
Folks reaching for the threshold
The unborn conceived
By the sign believed
In the star's story told
Which way to think and decide
What went wrong
For how long will it take to subside
When the dead can't even rest

Hear confirmation others business's
What will curse and who will confess
To pass the oncoming test
All is revealed by light
You never really can sow
With a river that flows
In every direction by twilight.

The Reliable One

A survivor, a stimulator,
An original originator, a real creator
Dreamt for the masters in the middle of the night,
And robbed Peter to pay Paul.
So darkness turned to light.
Now he's a legend of the fall
To a thousand points of delight.
He takes the sweet lady of the night,
And turns her sorrow into Snow White.
Whatever he does, whatever he gives
He makes us live in the way it was,
Because he really knows us.
He's a tribute to the root
With leather gloves and black suit.
No jewelry to shine with his black boots.
At everything that is bright
He's a gentleman of the night.
The stars are his compass
He's always among us.
Or around the next corner
Up the street
The quiet stranger you once in a lifetime meet.
Polite and generous
If you were to greet him in his bashful manner.
A prince, a spirit, a helpful, kind sir
Did he not offer food and drink
In the holiest grail
Where light and darkness
Left a bloody trail.

Food for Thought

I bit my tongue today
Reminding me to be thoughtful
Before I say something that comes
Faster than a dart from a gun
I can't excuse it away or say
I was kidding or trying to have fun
Then it started to bleed that reminded me
Of the possible seed I could plant
A conception before birth
How the unthoughtful words
Could bruise a heart torn
When it's too late you can't take back
No matter how bleak something was said.

I bit my tongue today chewing on something
I dare not ever say
Food for no good thoughts in mind
Rather go hungry, sleepless or go blind
When I think about how unkind it would be
If no hesitation or meditation could stop me.

When Love Is Gone

No more art
No more beauty
In her heart
No more, said she
When love is gone.

Day is ended
Sun has set
Moments lost
I now regret.

Where have you gone
My only love
You and you alone
Create the masterpiece from above.

You gave your heart
You gave me art and beauty
You alone broke my heart, said she
You and you alone.

Night stood still
Brow damp wet
Chances I had, I can't forget.
In my loss, she tenderly laments
Of chances that came and went.

Now days so long
Darkness fills silent clouds
Hides the memory of thee
Where emptiness surrounds.

I curse the day
I was born to believe
Love would stay
And never leave
When love is gone.

Than I Ever Been

Now
I'm going out
To go back in
Farther and farther
Than I've ever been
Clouds form and
Now breaking
Up into symbols
In my mind
As the smoke clears
I became all ears
And saw
What I heard
I was swallowed up
By the bird in my hair
And then
Flew farther and farther
Than I've ever been
As I go out
Only to return again
And lay by
My dreams
Where I once
Use to float
Into where
Only I can go
My angels hold
Me
The masters
Salute me
The dead touch
And kiss

My head
As I bow
Before all
On all sides
Everywhere I
Turn
Smiling eyes
Greet me
As I go out
To come back in
With them
farther and farther
Than I've ever been.

The Prince of Wealth to Be

The prince introduced me
To the crowd
Because I was blinder than most
But he reminded all
I was educated by the sages
And was
Earnest of assured respect
So quiet was hushed
I began
To speak in the silence
That is all of ours
The thoughts
No words could utter
So kind
It no longer mattered
If I was told
I was blind
But I chose the harder road
To no longer beg
At the gate
Or to sit and wait for
Ears to come to me
Even though they were the things that
Made me see.
My heart chuckled
In the dizzying stillness
With my lids tight
I shared
With my lips
And
Down came her hair
I felt it with a slight twist

Of her interested, thoughtful head
From far away
Where now
I am seated, I stand
Internally naked
For all to watch the skeleton
To turn into seed
As each one dropped
Into soft, flexible ground of
Heart listeners
They, too, all had different
Views of their own clues
With shut eyes
And open ears
Began to see exactly how I did
I looked back as a kid
I heard myself open the treasures of
All the wealthy
I said
When it's too hard to try
Because you've been overlooked a thousand times
So easy to die
To let this life go by
You have a way out inside
With thee eye
That opens when
You decide
That there is always something more
Than the life
For how it really is
There is an afterlife
In this present time
That can
Be more than
What it is
But you have to point

Your arrow
In the direction
It needs to go
Only then will you know
That all your pain
And heartache
Was meant for you
The soul
To live and flow
To grow into another light
Be someone more
Than the one you used to know
Becoming the new you
Is what you are inside
I know you know this
Go there to where you are now
Let it all go
You are waiting for yourself
To take hold, to go on and be
You are the wealth inside that makes you free.

Behind the Curtain

Deny yourself, love one another
You need your brother
Thank you, thank me
What you have to do to be free
Wait for a sign
Read your horoscope
Be on time
Don't forget
To pay your rent
Watch the clock
Time well spent
Listen to this
Don't look at that
Happy people
Don't get fat
Do you remember
What he said
Skip a meal
Do your chores
Don't browse too long
In the stores
Write to them
Call for her
Do you think about
What you remember
Read this drink that
It's cold out, you need a hat
We can meet tomorrow night
Make some heat in the light
Where there is nothing within
Memories last
Hearts as one

Everything the same under the sun
We get whatever is coming to us
That's the way it is
It's the way it was
What one doesn't, the other does
Why?
Because
Yesterday, today, forever more
It's always the same as before
Surrounding changes on every shore
That keeps us here behind the veil
I like my time
Every day I give
A little more away
It never was mine to keep
When I bring myself back
No one can subtract
Any of the facts
When I finally go to sleep
Within, we all live
Inside one another's minds
From the windows on each floor
Unlocking the key hole of each gate
We all find ways to make it through
Every day we age a little more
But we renew with youth within
The neighbors think
Without knowing it
Till the end when it happens
No one makes a wish
Or feels a prayer
Till they admit
They're in there
Every night we go away
We come back before a new day
Where are all the questions

No one remembers to ask
Every day we turn the page
A little deeper into the unknown
But tonight with eyes wide shut
We can see all the seeds we've sown
In and out of doors
Passing through walls
Walking, crawling on the floors
My name
Someone always calls
Every direction I go
Is another place
Someone will look for
The unknown
We eventually let go
Must we always be
Broken apart
Where we once began
Deep down in the brightness of dark
Never go back
The same way you came
They may recognize your footprints
Or know your name
It might be a set up
Or a way they play a twisted game
Someone's out there
I can just feel them in the air
Ready and waiting
For you to ensnare
It's you, and they don't care
The enemy is quiet
Not moving an inch
Thinking you and I
Will do in a pinch
But we understand
Way too much

To embrace that shame
So whatever direction you take
Make sure
That the route you're on
Is not the same way you've been
As twilight draws nigh
The darkness kisses the day away
I begin to slowly go within
Creeping all around
The subtle takes hold
The night bends its bow
From one end to the other
End of the soul
You can feel it like closed eyes
Of the deep sky of red in the west
To the function inside my head
Leads me to my rest
My name is called
With a voice no one can tame
With everything in my memory
Still the same
Every day
At the break of dawn
I see a new creation coming on
Watch as I wait upon
The one is here and there
Its wonder is gone
Like the stars before the eyes
Walk through the morning skies
Up the streets to the sounds that reach
All-nighters' lullaby
We are new again
Give to live and love our life within
As we kiss good-bye
Another memory draws its line
It lingers throughout our time

Before we come together
Feed each other
The best that we will ever be
How heavenly we are you and me.

Spirit of Light

Spirit of love that drives away hate
Who kept me from my evil fate
That taught me the truth
My guide protected me in my youth
Who put the colors in the rainbow
That gave me light to my darkened soul
Who teaches eagles to fly
Gives peace to those about to die

Spirit who is gentle understands pain
Who created sunshine and also rain
That was fire in the night
Who helped me walk into the light
That moved on the face of the deep
My guide put dreams in my mind when asleep
That knows everything and is full of grace
Who comforts and exhorts through time and space

Spirit who will raise me from the dead
Who will lift me up from my bed
And place a golden crown upon my head
Leading me into eternity's realm
Gently placing my hands upon the helm
Where we will sail through the universal highways
The Spirit and I all the rest of my days

Rejoicing, evermore singing the glory of God
Ruling with peace and not with the Rod
In every palace dwells a son and daughter
Who drinks from the cool clear crystal water
Spirit who breathes on us everywhere
The breath of eternal life that's in the air
That gives faith, love and life
My spirit of heaven, my spirit of light.

Over There Is Here

You're mesmerizing music
To my ears
Your eyes touch mine
I see
The melody
That brings you tears.

I drink them down
In my soul
So you can live
And grow in me
With your mysterious
Sounding harmony.

That awakens all of life
Every time you're
Guiding on the wing
Of something
That may not
Ever be again.

In the quiet before night
I hear the gentle sighs
From those on the other side
Of here
For no other is there
Only here and now guides us.

To know your thoughts
As you
Read my mind
This is what you get
For being so kind
Your night contemplative dreams.

Many Untold Stories

Momma goes flying down the road
For her children and a pot of gold
They wait sitting quiet and still
Papa forgets again how she feels.

Hearts pounding across the lonely river
Sending messages no man can deliver
The crying dove or the howling coyote
The saddest eyes or the clear, crystal sea.

Many untold stories
Where are we inside?
No guts, no glory
Overlook your pride.

Strawberry blonde ivory fair
Racing down the way that's there
Nobody knows like a mother true
Going after her tender babies two.

Way out under a starry sky
I'm walking down where I cannot hide
In the open air I'll be free again
This is my chance I know, my friend.

Many warm longings
Where she lingers
Tonight steadily sings
All the wonders.

Doors unlocked little, quiet girl talks
Her eyes are my skies that walk

Beside me in the cool, crisp air
As baby boy reaches and touches Mommy's hair.

One splendid night I conquered fear
Only because I thought you were here
Moon was full and bright was the night
Shedding halos around everything in sight.

Many old glories
Where we used to be
Many untold stories
Still linger in my memory tonight.

The Missing Piece

Feeling like an old
Wooden hash pipe
Burned out from Morocco
Who has not touched
My mouth in the trance
Of sweet tranquility sailing
Where eagles nest looking up toward
In way too many moons now.
But still there remains
Some resin left within
Just about then
She started cooking my brains
Quarter passed ten
To burn I myself in secret
By my ecstasy exit upward.
Be my own personal light
As ages roll on and on
I'll be gone—again tonight.
While the rest take their sleep
Out of sight
As I levitate in my float
Like light blue smoke
Swallowing up the heavens.
After all is gone
I arise into what
Has always been
The essence
Of the invisible weightlessness
That turned on its side
To finally be one
For all.
Falling out of bed

From being drenched
In her laughter
I was immobile
Inconsolable.
Jesus of the blue lapis
Where are you?
My heart is his,
She swam in my currents of tenderness
I wiped her off the floor
As the wall faced me
The door waited patiently
Falling through the ceiling
I left spontaneously
Above it all at zero degrees
I didn't feel a thing
But only me inside myself
Totally completely one
I of all.
I thought it
I was back in bed
With her—where ever she
Went I don't know
But all bodies asleep
Only to awake
Hand her my real hearts of skies
That never stays the same.
Now I've got to deal with
What's not yet
That sits without notice
By the insides of who
Swallowed the missing piece.

What Will Be Is Already

The dark is bright
In the construction of what will be
All is always completely known
In both kingdoms I share the throne
The essence of fiction is the blueprint
Of what you bring into your existence
Every world we all exchange in and out daily
We will deliver the stillness of the night
Into the exterior of what is happening
All beings are like thread being spun around
Where the breath flows out from the head
Any appearance of pausing is a phantom
A mirage that is an unconscious delay
For any on the other side of the mirror.
We are all split images of each other
In the stillness of the constant movement
That eternal breath of life.
When your sight is elevated and transformed
The unknown will never be pictured on the wall
Of your interior skull again.
The movement of measuring was the start
Once upon a timelessness
Where creator and created were first discovered as one.

Innocent Blood

Innocent blood dripping inside the slaughter mills
With your vacuums, needles, scalpels and pills
Robbing the fearful and irresponsible like big business
One day all will see the atrocity you've done by this
Like Hitler who believed in abortion on demand
I've seen the U.S. raising its own dictator's hand
Over the millions of babies slaughtered each year
Have we gone too far in disrespect of life, so dear
As we take away life that was sovereignly allowed
How can we turn and salute the flag like a hero so proud
You don't hear the screams an unborn child makes
Or understand the hell a mother goes through after it's too late
The world has been aborting babies before you and me
In modern times are we as blind as barbarians who couldn't see
Like King Herod of old who tried to abort Jesus too
Mr. President, how I wish I could get through to you
Joking and laughing at your parties making promises in your campaign
While unborn babies gasp for air slowly dying alone in pain
Many won't see many will fight and protest
When the guilt stored up in you won't let you rest
We should know better, but do we give a damn
About the unborn so many ignore as a sacrificial lamb
Well it's sure genocide that starts deep inside
Corrupting minds by men legally licensed to kill
In the end, taxpayers are forced to pick up the bill
Mr. President, how can I get through to you
Every aborted baby's blood is dripping off your hands too
Have you become so numb not able to see or feel
That what you are destroying is really real
All the lives that could have been
Are now voices of those crying in the wind
So let the winds of change blow

Those unborn babies' voices
Deep into the ears of those
Who will one day make the choices
Let the winds of change
Blow the truth deep into our ears
Let not history repeat itself
Like it has so many years
The conscience, tender, eternal, never meant to die
Is waiting and watching down deep inside
I have no intention on being harsh
Cause of what's been done
But in another time and place
I believe the innocent will judge one by one.

The Source

She laughed at
Her tears
As they gently
Rolled down
She went to the river
To cool herself
In the summer sun
True love
Is when love is gone
But we still by our will
Continue to love
She fell head first
But her thirst could not
Be quenched
She was steaming still
Too hot to touch
Every prayer—unanswered
At least that's how
It appeared
But still nearing the apex
Where we finally meet
Kissing the sunrise
In each other's heart
We speak
Never forget the true memories
We keep
Till we leave
For all true love
Is eternal
Where it always stays
We go there often
When we lose our

Way
The world only loves
You
When you win
Some say this is
The only love
That would ever be called a sin
Even if we
Have to start all over
Loving yourself
Is where I'd begin
For if we choose
To go within
Where you know
You cannot hide
That leads you in
The very moment you do try.
Cease to see
Your yesterday's mixed with your
Tomorrows
For today is the day of love
That erases all your
Sorrows
But if you fail
She heard without love
In its course
It is not in vain
The true love from above
Will love you back
To the source
In the pouring rain.

Calm

Calm
Move me along
Peaceful melody in a song
No thunder or bells ring
I could've looked at you
For days more than anything
Can wake me from
My slumber deep
Not forgetting to remember
Your dreams in my sleep

Calm
No restless honor
Can mislead or fail me now
I have light in peace
That will be how
I walk in darkness and see
Lying in your arms
Being truly me

Calm
In the storm that takes away
That which I held onto so tight
I am suddenly still
With no intention to try
Resting in my quiet with us
Like a warm, soothing balm
All is calm
In the peace I trust.

Frozen in Time

A swan
Floated as she walked
Gentle, placid atmosphere
Toward me
Like a fawn
Quiet, tender and stepping
Stillness, she hid in the wing
To myself eye to eye
The picture framed
Frozen in time
Matchless moment
That will never again
Replay the same vibes
I gladly lost myself
What the essence was
That she expressed to me
In a split instant I'm in it
Forget where the moment went
That we intertwined in
A piece to a puzzle
I'm in her field
Now suddenly more alert
Hopes and dreams mesh
More real than life
We become everywhere
Our worlds together
Whispered words to a prayer
From the hearts combined
Saying without sounds
But with lines in between
In the magic I did find.

Once

There's a place passed
Where no return back
To what was
Where there is no more
Do or die
And if you could go back
Like visiting your old
Hometown after many years
It would not be the same
As it was
For everything that was
Did what time always
Does
You can't get it back
All you can do is
Remember if you can
But not completely understand
Why it's not
Ever going to be like it
Once was
So if you're gone
And you don't know
Where to go
There you are now
Being in another 'once'
That'll pass on also
And be another place
You can recall
While you can't be
In the same once
In the middle of another again.

Mr. Home-Wrecker

Two squinting eyes a watching
Like a snake in the grass
Happy couples always thinking
Their marriages will last
So he sneaks around houses
He whispers on the phone
He slithers between spouses
To get inside the home

Mr. Home-Wrecker, you don't care I can see
If you're trying to destroy another family
You've not noticed now
This may be true
But in the end marriages and children
Will have the last laugh on you

You grin within
Like the devil in darkness you creep
Floating past the children
That are peacefully asleep
To twist thoughts and words
In a married couples heart
Bringing misunderstanding and struggles
To tear them all apart

Your time will come
No doubt about that
I've seen you wear many faces
Alone with your favorite hat
Having no heart or conscience
That's why you do what you do
Hating love and family and everything
That's true

You make friends
Influence with nothing but lies
Then you subtly slither in
Like a serpent so wise
Spitting destruction in the air
Drawing the prey unknown all the while

They ignorantly follow you with a
Warm, happy smile
Creating hard feelings
Alluring with your tricks
Bringing strife between husband and wife
That's how you get your kicks

Waving and winking
At all the parties
Always saying thank you and please
You never miss a beat
As you raise the blade to the heat
To sever another relationship
Just by the move of your poisonous lip
Or the twist of your fingertip
Into the eyes and hearts
Of the innocent

Unfaithfulness through lust
Is your direct source
To break up a home
With separation and divorce.

Forget Me Not

Barefoot standing over your tomb
Evening's wintry mornings frosty
Like the ocean where you sleep
Now your legs no longer run
To the rising sun
Over here on the other side
I'm standing here now
Your voice is a reminder
To the path
Back to where you are
Above the stars
And bleeding within
Down inside this ocean
Recalling days you lived in the womb
Now nights so dark and deep
I had dreams for you son
To my outstretched arms
The grass so much greener
I thought I heard you say
But my mind is in yesterday's tide
Like lightning and thunder
That leads back
Underneath a crown
Barefoot, waiting
I, too, will lay one day.

The Basement Boy

The lower I go
The higher I ascend
From where I was sent
Alone
There's no place like it
To fly through colors
With supersonic speed
I paid for loving myself
Till I make it
In the flowing liquid bliss
I'm gone
According to them
But I am
That's what makes this
So incredible
To be where I'm sent
The gift of gifts
That would lead me
Through the damp wet cement
I let myself go
From what was never meant to be
Living a new life
In someone else's history.
You know
When you truly have learned
You will stop your running
And be still
Knowing you will not be burned.
It's not easy to face
All your life for you
Is what you create.
But now you know

How your soul
Has brought you to this place
Of pure knowing
You can start watching
In the temple of your mind
All the thoughts
That you can use to build
A life you could never find.
No light
But what's in my head
Innocence in the basement
The boy who stayed still
One day
Far away
He'd leave without his will
To where and how
He never experienced before
All because of
The silence he heard
Inside
Alone
There's no place like it.
No one ever knew
What he lived threw
Giving up
Trying to remember
Not to admit it
No place known
The basement is my throne.

Living Her Land of Milk and Honey

Softer than warm milk
On my tongue
Almost as fair
Dripping, melting
Inside her
She lightly purred
Caressing every touch
Consumed we both
In total measure
I am not dreaming
Her flowing voluptuous,
Pulsating, meshing in our
No end
Timelessness, eternal love
We enter in
All over each other
We devour, absorb
True beauty of
Deliciousness
Of all the attractiveness
Reddening in the white
Sheets
All skin delicacy we claim
As one flesh
We gnaw, we bite
Gently rip in
Exhilarating desire
Clouds of pure fire
We roll, tumble through
Delightfully
Sucked till every
Drop was drunk

Knowing internally what we are
What we are doing
Is forever
A touch of sensation to
Keep reaching for more
Filling up the endless
Stream
We are the center of the
Universe
Bringing out all of ourselves
With a continuous gush
Ecstasy
I clamp on with drooling mouth
Intense hands with all ten
In precise motion of intense feel
Squeezing, titillating
Ripen our tender
Nerves as we pick
Shining
Her bodacious breasts
Billowing, branching
Bouncing amazingly
Before my eyes in my
Hands in my mouth
As she was so suavely
Craftily in her style of
Gladly, freely giving them
Up to mutual extreme pleasure
Then slowly, wispily letting
Down their creamy touch over
Hanging across my torso
I am flying in between
The big, huge girls with all
My heart's manhood
To drown in my thrusts
Blasting in sonic

Gorging
To roar cause in
Heavenly delights
Beyond words to speak
Creates forever.

Forgive and Forget

Week after week, night after night
You nag and complain
Till we have a fight

You sound like a broken record every week
You fill my head up with so much garbage
Till I can hardly speak

Now I didn't get married
To see what I could get
Or to watch you go into a fit
Or to have to babysit
Or to throw in the towel
And say I quit
If you need help
Then you should get it

I can't change the way you think
I can't change the way you act
Nobody can change anybody
And that's a fact

You try to corner me with your words
With your confusion that hurts
That only makes matters worse

It's a vicious circle
You want me to keep running round
That's making me lose heart
Making us lose ground
Someone has to forgive
Someone has to forget

Or we'll both end up
With only regret

No material gain, money or horoscope star
Can ever change
The way we are
Because we all have a time
We all have a number exact
And there's nothing created
That can ever dismember that.

Dust of the Earth

You call me a teacher
A walking mirror
That's true of you
Isn't that clear
On the crest of a wave
Where the truth
Has become too delicate to save
Its seeds are being blended
In the ground of technology
As the frightened future
Seeks refuge
In its own web of misery
No doubts, no clarity
The bubble ever expanding
Everything is twisting
As leaders like zombies
Constantly insisting as it turns
Before it can be understood
Or discerned
The real dream has been swallowed up
Gone—the only hope
For tomorrow
Is in the memory passed on
One soul to the next
At last the truth
Will spring forth
From the dust of the earth
The human race will learn again
What life was really worth.

When You're Not Ready

I didn't come here
To tell you
Even though you
May think so
It's been a long time
All has passed
As it did
When you were
Figuring how to make
Your great escape
Everything back then
Has remained—somehow
In all of our wandering
Though it has all passed on
We still—even if it be
Lonely in our
Dreams
To face the facts
What brought us in
This particular place
Now
Brick by brick
Block by block
They try to tear us
Down or Apart
But in the middle of
It all
We come to the one
Conclusion
It comes when
We surrender
To one another's

Embrace
And know
Right then and there
That what was
Has led us
To this overflowing
Lightning grace
To share and make
Us care
To be whole and
One again
This is why I came
Not to share in any
Words
That can neither
Explain
The blame nor the shame
That others have
Cast upon us
Some keep stuffing
It all within
No matter how much
It hurts
Until one day
They burst into
Flames
They have their own road
To find and
Understand
But now here
It's just you and I
Now together to
Make it right
Surrender to the
Heart that's from above
I didn't come here

To tell you
Even though you know I did so
If I waited here too long
It was only because
I just wasn't strong enough
To be in love.

No Longer Break

Time and Space
Has finally went astray
Besides it doesn't exist anyway
Stillness is where
You'll find out about that
And that sameness
Is the last ongoing tradition of men
That is falling
Inside its own hole
And history keeps repeating
As the blind
Loves to love
In its imagining
And everywhere
Anyone goes
Is where you'll find
What you think you need
It's always late
When you're drifting
And when you
Touch me before
I even get there
Nothing I can really say
My heart
Is beginning to awake
And the stars light their own way
Wondering what, kind love
Or anything else can do
Before the dawn of my soul
Rambles me through
The cleaned up alleyways
Of my memories
For a heart
That can no longer break.

All I Got

Death
Is the sting
That will bring
Everything
Into being
It is quicker
Than night
Stronger than dawn
Hotter than hell
More righteous
Than heaven
When we are gone
Nothing's right, nothing wrong
I can honestly see
Now that I'm older
The world in life
Has grown colder
What I learned
As a kid
Is do what my folks did
Do the best
I know how
Because all I really got
Would be right here and now.

He Was Just Here

Getting lost
No, I don't smoke
Being at the right place
Maybe love is with me too
The only ones that fit
Are the eyes in the leaves
I miss only
Though angels stare
What never comes back
Red rocks
The door is waiting and ready
The crack in the wall
Time is not time
There's always another place
The fifth wheel
Is behind the eight ball
Where I can't see me
From class to class
Inside
Now I'm awake
So tenderly disturbed
"Hey, you kids, get back here!"
If you can't find me
Can't sleep no more
Our time
We're leaving
The crystal jungle with closed windows
Loves the way you disappear
With his hair slicked back
Weather breaking up
River awakes
Deep in tears

I lost the channel
Eyes flutter
Moon brownish-yellow crescent roll
Dogs head up underneath heat pipes
Give a toast
When my baby's got a new hat
On each block
Damned if we do, damned if we don't
A tomboy's dream
Your neck is mine
I have to walk to stay here
Falling as I rest
Grill that log
My message in a bottle
Rush that hide
Silently excited unknown
Behind the davenport
Turn the calendar
Collectible coins
Sing low
She's giving me a sign
Salute the survivors
The world has washed up again
You are so full of what's in it
You can
Scrunched down so hard to it
Give me
Take me to the limit
With leftovers and hand-me-downs
Either way you are stretched
I be happy
I'll go do it all over again
Take me to a garage
To keep focused and give away
Sale.

"They Are You"

No places
Only faces
I've ever seen before
Who are they my Lord?
"They are you"
In my lying down at twilight
They came to me
One two three
One right after the other
No one I recognize
No one I memorize
Only you can tell me true
Who are they, my Lord?
"They are you"
Every one
Every time
I let them come
In your mind
I let you see
Each face clearly
So you'll understand
What you are
And what they mean
It's not hard
Once you ask
When they've been seen
Without a mask
By your eye
Within your mind
You never seen
Them before
But like a dream you forgot

A thousand dreams ago
They knew you
Somewhere sometime
Now that you care
They live now in
The picture memory
Of your mind
Who are they? Are they me?
They are you.

Angel in the Night

Shadowy light
through the crack of night
bangs a door
upon a hurricane breeze
while the second body
tries to leave
I'm trapped again
between awake and sleep
I want to go home
where ever that is
I will never be remembered,
but only by what this is
what is it to you?
you'll have to answer
your own questions
you can only deny
for so long a time,
but by then
I will be
where you
will one day see,
but afraid
now you are
for you do not
dream upon
the light years
of a star
for when you desire
and don't get
when you reach for
nothing is sent
lying waiting

in the night
the darkness will widen
and your crack of light
will be deciding
the sudden silent blast
in the room
stillness for a siren
that never blows
for you now know
that hearing is the last to go.

The Place Is You

You are the place
Where others think
You are waiting at
But none of that
Though you appear still in
Your place you are not
Nor were you ever
You place as your destiny
Is moving under your feet
Without your attention
And you are approaching
As you stay, entered into you
And as you create
As you always have
Your place expands, for more existence
That cannot be measured
In time or space
But only by the place
That is forever moving
Along where you dwell
You will notice that all that is
In you, from the past
All the way to where you are
Is all made up by and for you
For you are truly one and many simultaneously
You are a place that will become a place
For those who come to their selves
Like you loved unto you
And so on and on this will
Be all worlds' end
Universe begin and continue
The way, as all have, by you now

Remember gladly, you are a place
That always was, and always will be
You are a creator
And you are made up of
Your own creation
Of your own doing
With the All that always
Has and will surround you.

Awakening

She said my unconscious mind
Needed constant attention
As I let her awaken me once again
Out of waters unclear, dark and deep
That so peacefully and mysteriously
Roll in its sleep
My eyes moved back and forth
Like two birds flying across
The morning horizon
As she began to give me
That constant attention
Her voice like the sound
Of sweet evening breeze
Took me deep inside
Where my mind lived in perfect ease
Where was I? What did I have in store
She said things I never heard before
Like a foreign language circling the shore
Where I asked for more
As she began to open another hidden door
A voice whispering saying
"The end is never really the end
It's just the start of a new beginning
I felt the hidden, mysterious glow
Of a perfect, round moon
Coming through the window
In the lonely back room
Where no soul's ever been
That's where I began all over again
To finally awaken
For my inner eyes to see
That I was in love with myself

As she showed me all the beauty
That wonderful light shining at life
In waves of glory flow
Passed the silvery night
I was awoke in the silence of tranquility
As she held my hand
Then up came we
Both of us together
From down deep out of the sea
Awakening me.

Unturned

A shower came
outa my cap
as the towel fell down
on the cat
that jumped so high
even the rainbow
had to duck
as all the colors
squeaked and quaked
melting together
as one
the big, black hole
that never really dried up
in the sky of hope
where her two sisters
faith and charity
dated me
aha, I never felt
more sacred than then
when I cleaned up
the whole mess
with no beliefs or love
I did it all by myself
alone
as I left the stone
unturned
I would never be
burned
again and again for
all that mattered
was
how to forget about
all things — that really
won't ever mean anything again.

Take Myself as I Am Now

Making me wonder again
Why you took me in
Then to say in the end
I don't want you at all
The crazy thoughts
That circle my mind
Are strong enough
To make the wisest man
Go blind
When all your life
Is from pillar to post
You don't have
Anything to put on your toast
All you think about is
The one you want to
Love the most
Cause all I remember about you
Is the happy goodness
That now has left me too
The wicked thing that makes the
Darkness sing
Is towering over me so tall
I've got to take myself as I am now
Alone
Or don't take myself at all.

Ancient Vision

I envisioned in day, I envisioned I saw
St Peter in waves with wet bearded jaw
Nets wrapped tightly round each arm
Exhausted fishermen from the farm
Saying to everyone including me
Lay down your memory
There's no pain in feeling love
As I continued to drift back
When the saints hid in subterranean chapels
While the world slept in its private hell
They moved quietly like they should
Hiding behind a monk's hood
Singing softly their fervent prayers
Incense and candles filled the air
But I was assigned a stay-behind spy
In the enemy's territory
Like in the days of Augustine
When Rome was falling
Drums beat flutes played on
Feasts of fishermen last till dawn
Smell of smoke heat of fire
Crackle from salt oceans grave we admire
In telling you this, so the truth won't be missed
Lay down my brother your memories
When we hid in secret places
And trotted on rooftops
We ran in summer breezes
Taking chances calling the shots
I remembered what was said
On this side lay down your nets
Do you love your Master with all your heart
Who has called and set you apart

Fish for men who walk on dry ground
To lead them in like waves from the wind
To where they may be found
There are many who are in need even now as they sleep
If you truly love me, you will feed my sheep
For all that is left hiding behind these
Are the memories of their enemies.

Set Yourself Free

One glistening moment in the sun
Is over when the race is won
But before you start in time
Till the very end
To endure the worst pain of all
In knowing what might have been
One fleeting chance to challenge
In the melting years of your youth
But before you start deep in your heart
You must be ready to die, is the truth
Obligation shrinks the heart-felt desire
To do its best
But when set to be free
It will naturally be a victory above the rest
Wish I could go back and still be around now
When originality was easily found
Because there's nothing new under the sun
And anything that could be done
Already has been
So there's nothing left, no not one
So at least before I leave, let me know
More than I believe, because it's experience
That helps and makes the most sense
Out of all of the things that kept me on the fence.

Clueless Reality

No traces of what was
Society groping or
History books never told
Medicine is a misfit
I want to go back
To see when
You were
Every vision
Came alive after
The memories hid away
Only tomorrow tells
About all you forgot
Only desires come
When you have room to fill
She created what I can
Imitate for all that need
Never mind the times
Once again
What you say I am
On a windy, dusty
Torn newspaper street
That no one does anymore
I'll wait in my nook
I'm figurative
Breathing is for livers
Now the moon
Greetings
Sorry about what?
Your lines can't make you whole
Two years almost drowned
Why would I come
To the red night again

Don't try so hard
Living is easy
When you pretend
He was here
She took him away
If you're lucky
You'll turn around
Giving a light
To a
Stranger.

By the Old Moonlight Window

They take their lives—every day
After many prayers ago
And never knew
They would live to tell
The tale like they do.
I left my own unknown
To dwell inside
Somewhere down the road.
All the rest of life
Someone will tell how
The missing
Became the pieces
To the invisible now.
Every moment
Between now and then
Is the closed opening
Where we understand.
Not the paper
Or the ink, not the ring
And the celebration you think.
I want ours
To be
More than you and me
Whatever
Unpredictable, nontraditional
Can bring
Because it is beyond
The bond
That gives life
To the living
Leaving all your memories
You used as tools

In the cradle
That stopped rocking
By the old moonlight window
Where the branches
Break free a top the river bed-a-glow
No longer gives
What lies still
So now my lives
Rest as one.

Visions of Power

Visions of power
Searching for dead end men
Who possess nothing
But ready to be
Raised up again

To receive suddenly
What they cannot see
Or believe the unknown
It's changes that make men free

To be lead toward a life
Above the path that brought them down
So that they may see
Through the darkness that's all around

Visions of power
Aim with precision and light
While dead men wait
For their last chance in the night

Thoughts that burn
Like a furnace of fire
Wage war whenever
The other side gives a desire

To dead men
Who have nothing
But a place to die
The earth is filled with them
Who could've been saved
But never survived

You men of death
Nowhere to turn
The death of darkness
No more burns.

You that crawl
Gasp for air
Eternity has come
To deliver you from the snare

Shine forth with brilliant light
That rescue you
In the darkness of night

It will come
As you walk by the way
The sun lights the day

In remembering
The days of your youth
Thundering, rolling ways of truth

Coming to you now
In the moment of power
Disappearing every cloud
Lightning will guide thee by the hour

No eye can see
What you have brought before me
For your life is in secret

To those who say they know
You will pass the message on
That has been present from long ago

No more death or end
Go free and see
You've been raised again.

None Greater

In fading time
For love is more than love
When it's not there
Take my hand
If you dare to be real
In that moment of touch
Life takes on
A brand-new memory
That no sight or light
Could ever forget
And never deny
When the blind
Lead themselves
I see it could be
The dearest love
I could ever possess
Willing to take the hand
Willing to fall
Gently reaching out
Despite the risk
No greater love ... than this
To sacrifice the heart.

Ageless Conquest

Trapped
By time
Now leaving up off the lawn
Drifting in peace, to keep it
You must be blind
To have faith
You must know, to see it
Up to where my spirit is
I'm as light as a feather
No longer stuck in clay
They say hold on to
What you believe
I say give it away
You take your breath
Down and over
To the core
Everyone
Is unknown to themselves
Till they leave time
For a while
Finding out more
Than they ever knew
About what it means
To be really you
All of us
Without the denseness
In its place
I heard
The next floor up
Is getting too crowded
No wonder the mystery
Is becoming unshrouded

But I must leave
This temple
To get to my
Highest and best
For the open door
Is my sword
Making my freedom
Easy to choose
It's pointing to go
Into that direction
That's where it all got
Started
Before everything began
I'm still within my will
Attached to my sacred cord
If you do
Then you will allow life
To truly live
What more can one give
In a fading time
Such as this.

Vague

How you feel 'bout me?
Same way you feel 'bout me
Why you ask?
My dear, because I detect
You're wearing a new mask
It causes me fear
So am I to blame
For your fret, my dear?
I really don't know
Just yet sincere
Well, does it make sense
Not to fret till you know for sure?
Yes, I guess, well, will you?
I think so
Now look who's wearing
A new mask, my dear
Yes, and it feels good
To breathe again without fear
Wondering, worrying
There 'n' here
Everywhere I go I can know
When I change the mask
Of my soul
Come on darlin'
Let's go home.

My Loving Darkness

In my loving
Darkness
So quiet and still
A white light
Shines above me
The love of
Two
As united as
One
I do easily
See
In the darkness
Unlike the blindness
Of day
Where I cannot
Hide
Up goes the
Cat
To the ledge
After she scurried
To spy out
The night ... ahead
All is clear
With changing
Pupils
They dart at the
Slightest
Until total darkness
Over takes the
Dusk
Listening to you
Becomes

Like the needle
On the circle
Go round
My heart hears now
The music
In the darkness of
The moment so real
A century ago
Playing softly
The I ... am, myself
Only me
In the wandering
Above
The sound
Where I no longer
Breathe
In my unconscious dreams
I never lost
My way
Without total
Sight
I feel
As I floated in
Lifeless wind
Unknown to me once
Again
In my loving, darkness
Night.

Not So Fast

Questions will be asked then in time answered
By the decisions that bind the forces
That will have occurred
All things will happen just as they do
For they, us, and you
Will have to decide apart and together
And time will be taken up
By what we ourselves eventually choose.
From the churches to the bars,
From the moon to the stars,
I just can't relate to what is not ours.
I have no interest in thinking
What is right, what is true,
Or for those who care to think so too.
I only think about what is best
For me and you.
What a crime it is to throw away
Something for nothing,
And live the life most do.
Not being a fake does not mean
You have to be a martyr—
You can always tell a person's heart
Not by what they do or don't do,
But by the ones they choose to hang with.
My true friends are invisible before your eyes,
But unlike you, they wear absolutely no disguise.
I know one day you'll realize,
That there are no permanent good-byes.
Though you may grieve for a season,
We never really leave, and that's the reason
We have joy, we have hope, we have each other.
For the Light is our day and our night.

Walking the walls, hiding in halls
Looking for easy ways to slip through the cracks.
In and out we go, like no one will ever know.
We sure don't have to put on a show.
To get us to where we want to go.
The world can wait, but you and I can't.

Everything Is Good Laying Down

The light is fading
In the subtle mist
The music softly plays
Like her tender kiss
The sky is moving
To the romantic west
My homeland sacred
Cries who's the best
Everything is good
When it comes
Out of nowhere
By the time I'm there
River's moonlight
Takes me down
An unknown road
Will never die
Before the light of life
Flashes by
Growing slowly in the heart
Of a new born poet
Who leaves behind
Something he can't define
It's all in line
With the time that shines
The awakening dawn
As he stands
With stretched out hands
On the dewy lawn
Where Mother Earth
Kisses him once again
In the warm June breeze
He prays and suddenly

Everything breathes
Alive and free
Like a new world has come
He feels
He's not the only one
To enjoy the sights, the sounds
The lights, the rounds
Of energy bouncing off
His imagined inner light
That says
Welcome, enter
Come in, all right
You are the light
The salt
So bright
In you no fault
Drink my soul, I say
Eat the meat
That made the light of day.

Down the Hall

We were bright
We were young
We were heroes
That were unsung

As we traveled
With ease
I saw in your heart
A gentle breeze
I kissed
You by the trees
Then we fell down
To our knees
Because of it all
As we took heed

The stars
Were shining light
Glittering
Like pebbles of love
In the night
You took me by the hand
What could I say
When you said
Nothing can ever end
In the way
This is where it all began
On a bridge in the night
By the cool, golden sand
It was there we understood
All that was sacred, all that was good

As the kitchen smells
Linger down the hallways
I'm thinking how sweet
You are to me
I'm thinking again
How it used to be
Some say it's a tragedy

Others say it's a mystery
Never meant to baffle
Anyone's mind at all
It just occurred to me
As I watched you down the hall

I took a straight shot
For the only exit I knew
Then somehow the smells
Of the kitchen
Have a funny way
Reminding me
Of all the words
I shouldn't say

On a newborn
Spring day
The kids were
Out to play
When I heard you say
Let's give it all away
Now that I still
Remember so clear
You took away my fear
How gently
The day did fall
As I followed you
Down that lonely hall.

Down and Out the Side Door

Out the side door
Down the back street
I've got a weird feeling
You really meant it
Where the will
Ultimately leads
Hangs like a cloud
Just above the head
Ready to drop
Its petals or its bombs
On the night
The only choice you made
Came true
Its rolling
Like autumn leaves
Down an eerie avenue
Or it's dripping like honey
Off her lips
In a dim lit living room
You have not
Truly loved
Until you love
The unlovable
We prove ourselves
As we mark our space
Playing in the dirt
The only time we
Really know
Is when we hurt
We know so much
Before we came
Now that we're here

We gain
So much
That blinds us
From the plans we had
To be who we really are
Now another life
Injustice
Surely did dream
The anguish on the faces
Didn't have the strength to scream.
Too much to see
The truthful and honest
Have to work hard
In order to rest
While the vicious go free.
That's the story
Of time in purgatory
Not anything more
Than a life of work
With pain in a corrupt society.
Some call it religion
Others call it fate
I call it
Hell on earth again
For those who must wait.
This may very well be why
We have to talk it out
If it's true that we do
Become parts of the things
We complain about.
Never let the pillars
Be built higher than
All the wealth
You've ever seen
Completing the odyssey
In the unseen scope.

I will drench myself with all
Those who connect
With the source
Of all that is.
For I didn't mean to hurt your pride
Or meant to go too deep inside
The things from my head
Were obviously shed
You tried your best
But couldn't hide
By the time the sun came up
We were both fried.
Street lamps go off one by one
School kids bicker and make fun
Openness will bless
Places to go, things to win
If you undo nothingness
Make you healthy or look better
Treasures will emerge
With some sort a magical cure
Tenderness will surge
I don't waste my time with
Those who won't care
Nothing will be meaningless
Like ever before
Therefore another lifetime
That's all within
Not mine to share
If you quit
You can hang out on the edges
To open the door
But you won't come too close
When anything is too much
Of a good thing
Is never a waste
Too much whispering

Not enough secrets
No more mystery
Only exposed regrets
Drop down, reach out
It teaches you
What it's about
Everyone knows tenderness
Is true success
Always passes the test
Also gives you rest
Right or wrong
Shallow or long
Limp or strong
Nobody can see or get along
Without this I must impress
Upon the need of togetherness
That lies within
It's been always ever since
I figured you knew
It has no twin
But alone giving again
Covering a mountain
Crossing a river
Forgiving sin
As so many cowardly deliver
From heartless men.

You Can Stay

Dear love of mine
Connecting my thoughts and feelings
In my mind
Desiring as I plan
You can stay
Where no one can
Find the time
That always slips away
Dear life of mine
Bringing together
This golden chance
My ears to hear
My eyes to see
Into a love
For both of us to be.

Dear father of mine
You've been here
All the time
You make this love
Deep like the fire
That no one can extinguish
How you grant my desires
My very wish
I know the signs
How you draw
To what I think
How I feel
Together in my unspoken voice
To make my light inseparable
To my love's desiring choice.

The Magnifier

In my hand
I have an instrument
To help me peer and see
The things that are darkened
By the lack of light
That does not come in
It's bigger, it's clearer
Makes whatever I'm looking at
That much nearer
There's really nothing invisible
It's there to see
But is not
Without light
That keeps it from our sight
The magnifier
Opens doors and lets
The lights go on
Like streams of brightness
That shoot out at dawn
Amazement, magnificent
When we finally see
The things we didn't once before
All because of this instrument
Was overlooked
We could've seen more
Everything can be visible.

A Christmas Eve Night

Family and friends meet
Celebrating all that is good
A Christmas Eve night
With renewed brotherhood

A blue spruce sparkles
A fragrance all its own
Four Christmas angels guard each heart
In this historical home

The warm bread is broken
The sweet wine is poured
The old nativity scene
Still brilliant and adored

The fire crackles and glows
Chimney smoke rises into the cold wind that blows
While candles melt quietly
Shining through the windows

Here comes my Christmas gift
Isn't she a delight?
With smiles and sweet laughter
We reminisce a Christmas night

Young gals wait on tables
Elderly gentlemen read folklore and fables
A little boy turns the music box key
Mozart begins to play, it's time to dance you and me

Christmas is going to give birth
To another wondrous story tonight
And tell us all about
The one sacred light

Deep silence reminding all what was
It's Christmas! It's Christmas!
There's more to this night
Than just us

All of our loved ones are praying
Gathering grace to go up higher
As my love and I drift asleep
By the warm, peaceful fire.

Twentieth-Century Indian Upbringing

When I was a school boy
Unsure of you, unsure of myself
Silently asking for somebody's help
But never got any so now I understand
Why it's so hard to see, for you and me

So they put their thoughts deep into your head
Till you believe in something you can't see
Standing at the foot of your bed

They laugh at your imagination
They joke about how you feel
By the time you're a teen
They send you to a specialist
To try to understand exactly what you mean

The so-called wise is brought low by the mind inside
A teenage shadow that won't stay for very long
He's beginning to see, but all he thinks about is what's wrong
He can hear adults mumbling something
That doesn't mean a thing
Watch out for this, watch out for that
Your clothes are getting old, you're starting to look a little fat

As the boy approaches manhood
He ponders the things he would do if he could
Like he wants to or he should
With that thought, he goes to sleep till he floats into a dream
Where he meets a darling strictly from heaven
Who is seeking the same thing
His heart's true love; he hears her in the distance
Crying like a mourning dove

And the tears he hears reminds him of his past
The uncertainty was buried by the sudden blast of changes
That could not be stopped
That had to come to each and every dear one

We are soldiers of innocence born on the fence
Staring at our forefather's spirit who survived by living in tents
And God giving them reverence for you and me
It's been a long, long time since we were free.

The Transition

It was the transition
from my toxic world
into the beautiful
home inside my heart
as I awaken to this healing
bliss
I could never be mistaken
again
where my new world now exists
in the arms of love
I always wished
to be in
as I'm coming toward
and
leaving something even
better than this
I know
my home away from home it is.

Wake Up and Go to Sleep

Shadow boxing at dawn
Nuns one by one
Kneel before lit candles
To the new world to come
Doors unlocking
Cats at the window
I can feel again
As I come to myself
While fathers put out
Last cigarette butts
It's Tuesday
Momma's gone to work
Apples green from distance
Sweat rolls down his back
Alarm goes off
Every animal stretches
Accept us humans
Halfway between
When we all stand
The music of life
Reaches out to remind
Everybody is coming
What else can we sing
In the colorless season
That shines upon us
Grab hold of hands
Realize deeper than before
The clouds are outnumbered
As all the stars keep score
Say goodnight and go take a swim
It's not as far as you thought it was
In the instant

We forget something
To let us know
There's more to it all
Then look back
To say how change is so true
You read me well
Chances present themselves
Do you care enough to follow
In the circles that
Are being hit hard
She rises when it's over
He wipes up the blood
The moon is out so early now
Must be time to eat
Take the oxygen for granted
Always depend on beliefs
They are a cover up for insecurity.

Before I Was Born

Coffee gutters
of creamy diligence
no time to go
but now
the air is
sterile here
where only nothing
arrives on time
o day
the clock falls
no matter what
the web of
misery
cannot will not
get us all
for we are
made of stone
that blew out
from the core of the
woods
all the billions that
crawl
will at least remember
mmmm ... mmmm ...
good to the last drop!

Broken Sheep

I see the world
A graveyard
A tombstone of all the unknown
Died broken, cold and hard
With eyes shut
Looking straight up
Lined up in a row
They fall into the ground like snow
I have to dig your ditch
Cause you were born so rich
Lifeless without a breath
They talk, walk and hurry
To their death
Will there always be someone
Left to bury
Rick, Bob, Joe and Mary
I see the world
In its prophetic hour
Like a mad animal
Alone in space
Looking for a trace of power
To dig its own ditch
But it's too late
There's already been a switch
No life no more
It has come
How all we see
Is the world ... waiting to be
Buried like a seed
Stars will sing
Bells will ring
You will give me

Everything
Horses will run
Love is fun
You are
My only one
There's a heart
That beats slowly
Alone and cold
Without any light
The breath is deep
Awaits a change
To move on a call
From some forgotten soul
In the middle of the night
Everyone's asleep
Except the hearts
Who journey deep inside
The hide of the broken sheep
Who lie awake in the dark
Without a flicker of light
No one will hear
Their hopeless prayer tonight.

Left Unattended

You end up
in a variety
of mirrors
it's only as clear
as you've learned
sincerely
if you want
to go
you can't leave
till you figure out
what this is all about
to know
the only way
won't come
if you pray
you'll remember
things that you thought
were over
but they are all
pieces
that created this scene
of imaginary difficulty
that only you
can be
that no one else
will ever exactly see
the same
as you do now
it's not a dream
it's you from within
reflecting face-to-face
everywhere all around you

as you spin
you have to learn quickly now
how to settle down
to control and change
the very images with new ones
to give you a chance
to escape
this is where
you end up
when in your time
no attention to your
mind
all its
conglomerations
of unspoken changes
unrealized arrangements
you've done
without dealing with the
facts far away from
your heart's truth to love.
every time
you left behind
another denial undealt with
you add another mirror
that
you have to peer into
before you
can set yourself free
from you and
not me.

Another Train

Love and truth
The eye does hold the key
To live, to freely give
Not ask why
Is the opening door of what will be
When you don't even have to try
Life makes me feel
Like I'm waiting
For a train
My heart in her earth
My mind
In her clouds
Whispering things
Lost and wander
She was lightning one night
I roared like thunder
As all my lions awoke
Inside the castle I felt
God in my soul
Then the train came
It was time to go
I wouldn't wish
My life
Or my existence
To my worst enemy
Though now they both
Became my only friends
As all the world can see
I died in meadows
I arose in the rain
I took you by the hand
We rode the midnight train

When they took me away
You were asleep
By the prayers they pray
Old fashion crystals
Sparkle in your hair
Like morning dew
Against the shimmering
Dawning—where heaven shares
In our presence
Fading in the light so true
I fall into
Loves heart again
Though now they are
My only friends
I'm traveling back home
To you.

Facing the No End

The most real
To me
The deepest I feel
When I see
Facing death
Of a love
A brother
Death of a
Friend
Nothing else more
Than the
End.

All that Can Be Was Put in Me

Myths and magic, faiths, and creeds
Blessed, holy seeds
Gently throughout my visible life
Philosophies and prayers
Ghosts, spirits and love
Present throughout my sacred journey
Meditations and contemplations
Thanksgivings, ideas of the living
Throughout my soul's learning
Consciousness and colors
Cards and infinite numbers
Define my mind through
Winters and summers
For me to be among the chosen few
Invisibly no one disagrees
Visions, voices, apparitions and phantoms
Dreams that are buried forever in memory
Endlessly in the vast reaches of the stars
Water, blood and movement
Spirit and lovemaking
Hands reaching up as we go down
Under where our temples came from
Where no pain can remain
Only a continuous gathering
On and on like diamonds
Before an infinite sun of being
For us all.

The Visitors

Looking through my mirrors
Into the other side to see
Gazing passed the future
Through my fears
I guess they're just happy
To be with me
Perhaps
There's a lot of things
That I know
That I don't know I know
You know? My visitors
They come one by one
To tell me so
Into the night they creep
By dawn they're fast asleep
In my hands
Their souls I keep
Into their spirits
I plant so deep
All the wonder
That makes it hers
One night in my light
She's my little visitor
Apart from
All the smart and the dumb
Visitors I know
I guess she just loves
To come by
With her diamond eye and
Lay her head on my pillow.

Into the Other Side

Hopefully
the night be
for Halloween long and
far spent
with high-flying glitter
of wizardry dreams
of wondrous haunted memories
to be
in the right brain artistry
to the children and adults alike
who are starving
for the night
of the veil thinnest
to gather all the lovely
spooky ones
projecting out into new
worlds and dimensions of
adventure
in games and frolicking
there the lively ones
of cemetery ghosts past
on candlelit moon
above crumbling tombstones of
unexpected delights
of what will always be
world without end
the magical eternity.

Paradigm

She got the music
In her walk
She got the rhythm
In her look
She got everything
That women talk about
But they can't find it in a book

Magic in her smile
Sparkle in her moment
Quick alive beyond style
Takes her time, well spent

She's not preoccupied
With the obvious
Nor does she care
About what is rare
Or if her neighbors are jealous

She lives in a world
No one can duplicate
Because she was born that way
Her elevation from within
Makes her light brighter than day

And she leaves
Never the same way she comes
She could be anybody
She wants to be
Cause she knows no shame
Has no one to blame
Plays no games
She's her own self-lit flame
Glory is her fame.

If and When

They took what you had
they got what you want
their moving on
not waiting for any response.
everything's up for grabs
busting down doors, walking through floors
with flickering speed left and right jabs.
the bell never rings
they calculate their own time
to step aside—get ready again
arouse the eyes
where the entanglement always resides.
making the fearful society
more watchful
leading them into some unknown perfection
that only history really knows
if that will ever be,
or if we're all just here temporarily.
doing our time before
another door opens or shuts
or window smashed in
if we need to
truly have more guts
to face ourselves once more
becoming something else
unlike before
when comes the change
for the ones who are us.

Love Is

Love is quiet, love is frail
Love can grow and die on the trail
Love is tough, love will try
Only because love resides inside

If you love, you will see
That life came from love and always will be
Love is unnoticed even when it trusts
Love is hot, love is hungry
Love is reaching out to you and me

Believe in the impossible—Let it
Begin in your soul
Let love have her chance
Like she gave to you
Love remembers, love walks on
Love is in the air
From dusk till dawn

Love is scared, love is desperate
Love is full and will fill your net
Love overlooks, love gets angry
Love watches what will be
Love is a guest and usually alone
The love we have is rarely known.

Open up to the Night

Penniless and free
Always searching for me
Can you help
Just one more time
Before I fall asleep
So I can come
Up to where you dwell
No success in
Indulgence don't you believe
I've been in and out
But mostly on the go
If you can't find your source
Then look up
For your freedom
Falls like newborn silent snow
I don't ever worry
Nor will ever be led
To forget the debt
Because I have all my needs
Taken care of
With empty pockets
And memories love
With a smile
When the rich go by
I always know
Where to go
And what to do
With my ear
Laying on my heart
With my eyes closed
My side by side friends

Always there making sure
That I have come to the place
Where I can be
Opened up to the night.

Dwell Upon the Well and See

So much we don't know
So much we don't see
Little by little we keep growing
Toward what we will be.
This is our place, our call, our journey
This is our fate, our path, our destiny.
When it ends, no one knows
Will we come back again on another road.
This is our sentence for being in time
We don't remember asking to be here
Perhaps this could be our crime.
For we create our reality
Every moment we got
We do it by dwelling
Upon any particular thought.
I'm going to go
To all my favorite spots
Visit all your kids and little tots
And chase them all over the lawn
When they say I'm gone.
I'm going to touch your shoulder
For a gentle reminder
Whisper in your ear
To be a little kinder
As you walk through town
When they say I'm no longer around.
The sparks of life sizzle
Around my outreached hands
To lay upon all those to come
From foreign lands.
Pay more attention to your faith
Than your fear,
And when you leave
You will be at peace when you are here.

Earth and Sky

I was knocked off my high horse today
As I fell in slow motion
I vaguely heard a thing amongst all the commotion
As I crumbled in my landing in the dirt of the earth
Right to the very edge
I caught a glimpse looking down upon the abyss
In the struggle with fear to not lose and fall
I did not want to end it all
Despite the overwhelming pain and horror I saw
Truth staring back at me
With no one else to help but myself
I realized I was not alone at this point
Reeling in my own gasping
For what seemed like years to know exactly who I was
In the stillness of the settling dust
I felt the presence behind me – hearing
"I am not who you think I am, nor a man or anything
Created but, the total truth of you."
Not to save you, but to reveal you to you
And as I turned in the silence that surrounded me
I slowly became enveloped in this quietness
In the presence of the truth of me that shimmered
Like a delicate light of lightning
Reaching from one horizon to the other
From pole to pole I saw the truth of myself
The very presence of my soul
Reaching out its hand with glistening love
And I stood like I never did before
For the first time I saw my eyes
Reflecting back to me my own pure reality
I realized like a sunrise I was the earth and sky
That day that did not lose heart or fall away

I know now I would fall a million times again
Just to know and see myself like that
When thee unknown before the end
And unplanned fall would cause you to see or realize
In my hope for you it would be
The earth and skies.

The Sign of the Cross

He was just eight years old
Sitting on his daddy's knee
Mother came in and asked,
"When would you like to eat?"
We said, "How's about six?"
Then we jokingly laughed and said,
"Whenever you want to, boss."
And at the supper table
For the first time I saw
The sign of the cross
Heads were bowed
Eyes were closed
But the smell of the food
Went right up my nose
I could not have been more thankful
Especially to eat
I felt so hungry
I could hardly sit in my seat
My Mother said, "Please slow down
There's plenty to eat."
After she said that
I understood what she was trying to get across
But I still could not get over
How before we prayed
Dad and Mom
Made a sign of the cross
From their forehead
Then down to their hearts
Then to both shoulders
It must be something you do
When you're older
It sure caught my attention

Like some mysterious, magical talisman
And here I was now so much younger
It sure had a presence
Like something you would do
To help you find your way
It was something I saw
Every day before we prayed
It felt like there was someone
Watching directly over us
As though we were never alone
Nor could we be lost
Something warm and safe
That came to me
When we did the sign of the cross.

Twilight Silence Speaks

In my quiet, lonesome time
I think and wonder about her
For days
Then she would
Gently come
As I sat still—my shadow
Growing in the beginning
Twilight—sweet silence she
Speaks
As a whispered love
In her dreams I come
As she softly remembers
No feelings can describe
Her tender words
I'm falling again
As life kindly waits
Leading us way back
When
Angels held me close
Kissing her
Was my light
That led us
Our moment return
In our quiet
Lonesome time.

All the Same

I've stared out my window
Till day turned to night
Prayed for those around me
Just like you told me, right?
Gone as far as I could
Without giving up
I gave what I had
When times were really rough
The condition
The world's in
Nobody can point the finger and blame
We all are responsible for ourselves
Because we all are really the same
No one can make up the time you lost
All along the way
Some can help you here and there
But it's going to be you and you alone
On that final day
When your time is up
Your number punched
It's time to check on out
These things I have spoken to you
You'll know what they're all about
So there is really no time to waste
No precious moments to just look at
To watch and slip away
Because not a soul can make up the time
You have lost today.

By Dripping Candle Lights

Tired of being treated like a
Criminal
In a world
That's trapped like a fool
I drift in and out
Just to keep my sanity
But the world looks at me
Sees someone it wants to be.

Where I'm at, no one can come
A place captured in the mind
A place frozen in time
Like a clueless crime
Fast asleep in a night so deep
A place you'll never find.

I see someone's dream
Going through the kitchen door
Somebody's been here before
But they are here no more.

I wish I could remember
Last December
When they found me on the floor
Kissing the footsteps
Of my unforgettable regrets
That quietly left for the store.

Life feels so slow
This is about as fast as
An old man can go.

Temporary moments
Days where night ends
Nights where day begins
The meaning of life
Explained again.

The wind wise as a serpent
The moon harmless as a dove
I have nothing to resent
With my true love.

The trees steady like a mountain
The stars flow
Like a crystal clear fountain
I'm seeing myself once again
Bolder than a lion.

My body's like fire
My spirit soars to the heights as

I travel the frozen lands in my sleep
Drinking the fine wine of time
By dripping candle lights.

Nobody Knows

When nobody knows you
Because they live in the dark
You walk alone
Like an empty heart
That's been abandon
Torn apart
Nobody knows
Who you are
When night comes
As you're feeling lonesome
You can't forget her
All you do is remember
During this empty, cold November.

To the Point

Be what is
Not what has happened
You are always present
I do have a conscience
Because there is light
All around me
Shining unendingly
There are thoughts, words
Of every act I make
Light speaks
Within.
The voice to the point
And always gives
Moments onward
I tap in when
My heart looks to itself
To consciously see
What is really happening
When I remember.
The temple of mind
Is driven by the one.
In balanced order
I am secure
I am one.

To Do and Not Know

Pieces to a puzzle
I don't possess
Mind fills up with words
To touch you
Like connecting dots
Between the lines
To know
I write what no one's ever heard
But still I do
Some come in rhythm by day
As we walk
We don't have to convince ourselves
Others come in the dead of night
There's no one else
Suddenly begins to talk
How this occurs I really can't say
I don't have to see perfectly
It's a mystery to me
I like it that way
In the time to become
What I want to be
With you
I hide my truth deep within
So that I may love
More than once again.

I'll Be Right Back

Riddle rhyme
Make up time
My own
Secret in
I sit listen
Quietly
Till I instinctively
Lead certain directions
Pen goes
Flows
Up down
To my mind's
Destinations
I hear music far away
Or is that the halls
Coming through
Any way
Listen again
Till ride upon
A what
Builds
All will
Something someone
Can use someday
If I don't
A pulse
Put down on it
Just need
I'll sit
Quietly again
I'm
As

Something that may write
Read
Today tonight
Maybe
Next week.

What You Don't Know Can Teach You

She said she felt like she was in transition
Ever since I've known her it seems to me
That's where she's always been

Always going somewhere
But never quite getting there

I think I met her on a trip going to a fair
I myself felt settled without a care

Her hidden melancholy was obvious to me
At least out of the corner of my eye

Everything I did she either let go
Or eventually denied

I was always heading toward some place new
She was unknowingly sticking around
Familiar ground she thought she knew

She played the role and played me too
But I loved her enough
She made it all seem like it was a dream
That would never come true.

But I finally awoke
Found myself practically broke
Now suddenly it was easy
To let her go
Another transition to my soul.

You Are Heaven

I visited what came
to me all over
at once
in the pure mirror
of total darkness
all my lives
as I lived
through myself right now
like I never was before

Here they say
he goes again—in sober
delights of wonderful ecstasy
of transparent true images
that holograms only dazzle
laugh to sorely be
like until it happens
for perfect beauty is also
non-connectedness
to my own
connection of it alone.

Let it be so.

Too Good to Be True

You're so bad, you're good
Almost too good to be true
You're so bad, when you're mad
It's a glad thing to see
What you can undo
You're so sad, you make me
Feel so bad
Like the beauty of blue
Misunderstood by those
Who I thought never would
The closer you are
The farther you feel by far
The more unknown I am
The more you don't give a damn
About what's good, what's bad
From your point of view
I'm so bad, I'm good
I'm lost always
In some sort a' way
On another beautiful, sparkling day
My kids grown 'n' gone
My parents too
Don't care about the clock
Or about anything
That anyone can figure out, speculate
Or find out what's new
Because you'll be like the rest and say
You're too good to be true.

I Am Sure

Many, many live my life for me
As I live through them
And if I see what they hear
In the very hearts of men
I know I'm somewhere near
Only to be gone again.

Don't worry, don't fear
I'm always right here
If you are where you are
Supposed to be
Everywhere you turn
You will joyfully see.

And if you know you
You'll know
That I do too
When and where no words
Could ever explain
My love for you like sunshine
Will wash away all of your pain.

And before the next time
Surface
Begins to
You may be with another
And notice
I will be a part of all of us.

And if I'm
There and you're not
I'm going to be doing the same thing
There is no difference
Than the whole world going round.

Try not to feel dear
A little too much
Because it's up to someone else
To find their own way
And maybe we'll meet
Before it's too late
And when it's not
We're going to be into something I'm sure

What Does It Feel Like

It's all a lie when they tell you
That you will die

You want what you believe even if
You don't think it's true

Believe in your lies good, bad or otherwise
Watching them leave each clue

You don't go away
But neither do you stay

Where is that place
In between time and space

You've been to the borderlands
Far beyond your dreams

With the help of some huge hands
Your reality was created by you in each scene

All things visible, invisible move constantly together
We're moving right now as I write and you read

It's all happening in that area between the lines
We listen and read where all creation and its design

Become a part of itself perpetually, just to be
We pass along the sentence of time
Of what it felt like, to be free.

Stays a Bit

Death like dusk
Is the blending together
Of all that was
All that will be
Light kisses the night
Now by the red violet skies
Forgetfulness hugs memory
Both go through one another
To where they will
Start over again
Death surreal silence
Like a newborn babe's
First sleep
Heaven stays a bit
We'll sit quietly by the sea.

Endless Muddy Trails

Will what you want, want what you will,
But in your busy activity
Remain perfectly still.
In the moment of intent
Is the instant, spent
On the grounds you stand on
Which are the shoes that helped
You walk there.

Breathe in breath blossoming as ever autumn sheds
From the sanctified unending—my touch
I read the last page to the beginning
Immediately known a head of time
What's to come
As the Hebrews write from right to left
I know the light is always in my head
I take you where I want to go.

I walk in between commas and periods
Back through myself and breathe
Once again there I've been
Another chance to send you a time
All have missed as I recall
The dear kiss that fell
As I allow my sentence to begin
Perfectly swift in my idle wandering.

An adolescent bedroom in the attic
A child my altar prison basement
Temporary for sure dampness filled my solitude
Everything apparent finding out as one drifts remotely
Completely into nothingness I quoted my little black book prayers

At nights full open windows, asking my favorite master
To come and enter my full moon soaked room.
Alas, a trance of beauty engulfed my treasured
Mental screen and there draped half expressed my
Future with sweating eyes paramount cinema
To the borders I ran dizzying to behold over and over
With all of me all over I was not done till the shoe
Let go.

By midnight dreamy readers rendezvous
Realizing my destiny peaking in the palm of my hand
Before me in a second REM I'll never forget
For it was what I was
My nature plan from brain to flame
I now lavish in the sands of time
Budding up new and old ashes to let her be.
Smirking between orange and black streamers
I tip my basket black hat at all the party goers in my scene
I'm decorated with the golden Celtic power four-pointed cross
Upon my blue chakra, below my chin of ecstasy
As my little flower girls chase the tabby in and out of
Furniture rooms—

Where air radiates the galactic tones and
Soon more of the unexposed to come
Minds wishing the truth where colors are much
Brighter in secret
I gulped her with all my heart
My might guzzling her sweet wine
That poured forth, I sank as I drank
Gorging sucked every drop till she was bloodlessly
Unconscious and I was out of sight
Staggering like a fulfilled passionate hurricane
Floating away in tenderness.

I break your fast

You eat my morning dreams
Opening I the dawning
Windows drop the dew misty seeds
For you to drink in the sunrise rains
To wash down all you don't understand
In the fields where
My twilight leaps forth a lucid train
Coming softly you do
I bathe you in heavens broken tears.

Releasing you from
All the years
Into moments of
Perpetual joy.

For always is the night time
You will always need you
And none else.
You are the perfect match
The perfect one for you
A million stories confirm this
You read before the water broke.
We love each other as we love ourselves
I need none of you as surely as you
Don't need me
And this is the total proof we love each other.

And if I don't, no one will
Ever know
I do not need to help or message or convince
The reader of their need for me,
For they never do—nor never will
I only speak in write
What is true, sure and just
Between us here and now
Especially as you have chosen
To read my writings now.

Love Is the Disguise

No looking back
Or ahead
The voice that appears
Before my bed
Strung together like stars
As we to the sun
Now over ten thousand lifetimes ago
I breathe
Into each one simultaneously
As though
I never had to leave
This is what I want
More, for us,
Than you and me.
Love is the disguise
You can't
Always feel or see
Like the invisible
Warm blanket
Wrapped round you and me
It's hidden in
The anger, the hatred
For it's in every emotion
That is negative
It flows in the veins
Of the deceased that now live
We take it for
Granted
And fool ourselves
That it's the smile,
The sweetness and
Joy

But we neglect
Without respect
The love that
Irritates and
Annoys.
The love that
Dwells in darkness
By no sparks
But by itself
It is
What hurts
So we can heal
It is the unknown
That the one-sided don't know is real
Entities
Swirling round all over
Some
Outside my door step
Some
Trying to
Bust through into my head
You can't stop
The birds from flying high
You can't live your life
With only one open eye
Everything that is you
Is the place
You cannot hide
When they say
Come on give this a try
It's only a matter of time
You'll realize
Who you really denied
Entities
On every side
Wanting to clean you up

Don't want your broken way
All they had is
All you got
Just a little bit of
Time
Just like a shot
And it's over
There you are
Who you really were
Inside yourself
Now you know
For sure
Don't let anyone
Rob you of your
Own sacred discoveries
Because no one owns
Your keys but you
You came here alone
You'll depart
The same
You'll have all the help you need.

When the Breathless Still Mind Leaves

The dense heavy, spotty black
Floats real slowly
Up down across
The darkness shield
Covering mirrors, clocks,
Windows
Upside down flowers rot away
Ignorance unaware what's
Really there
Life in the appearance of death
The deep blackened sky
Consumes all the colors of the rainbow
Cry temporarily hid
Inside the mind of man
No one speaks or eats with
Doors locked, candles unlit
None moves
Where they sit
It's a pit in a witless wit.
Like a picture
Jailed in behind an
Invisible veil
Frame that bears no
Name
No one knows when it's a
Suspicious superstition
For all time never be recalled
To the very beginning that
Never finishes its ending
In the unsatisfied memory
Dreams
Like a snowman forever frozen

In a timelessness
Ever since you left
Bleak was the door
Skeletons keep closets shut
Brown dry flowers came
Knocking
In the empty arms of an
Imperfect unknown stranger
Staring off into the
Shadows of the cold, dirty
Purple moon
Where no one dies—
No hours in a day.

Steep Deep Slowly All over Hearts

Steep deep slowly
All over hearts
That blast to sound
Horns hollow last it all
Soundless sound moment
In the grains grove of the fiber
We breathe as we eat
Pure sun rays in air
Her silence swells my touch
Gathers the charms in one place
That always continues growing
In the visible clouds
Till dusk we pray ourselves
To deeper slumber
The waking eye knows
Floating upon her warm softness for me
Way above answers many do seek
Where roll and tumble in our
Pure laughter will lead
Only you walk along with me
As gracious fair necks call out
For my sky-blue heart with many
Tongues fever pitch above.
Loves depth imagined emotion surrendering
Over as the rest remain to be seen
All the desired tasks so easily done
All that reaches out
Eyes gleaming for a morsel within
Not one place nowhere will do without
Alone the solitary writer wonders does
This exist anywhere
Life within itself breathes its own to be

To move on as one talking to me
As my true self
Even though I'm my own worst enemy to
The end.

The Unrealized, Noticed

The unrealized, noticed
A familiar steps into
And through my door
A failing cheap
Acceptance
Many can't tell
Lay bruised
From sought after the gentle
Killers, of lonesome smiles
Garrison's about thresholds
The holy sounds treasured
By the waiting subliminal
Reversal capturing eluded
Fear
That tries but cannot linger
In line with the high sigh
Of their own
Internal bribes
White dark light is used
To brighten softness the cause
Presence tried past emergence
Toward a subtler rejection of
The cat's intense staring eye
Who is another in another spirit
Wholeheartedly no not frightening
Itself be said
As flying into the
Face
I close the
Door
And walk upstairs
To continue
Where I
Left off.

The Prayer

Let me breathe in the air
In my heart
So I can care to know
The highest good in all of me
Let me feel what is real
So that I can be my true self once again
Please don't let me be buried
In the grave of my soul
Let me live in life in the light of its love
That makes me want to live again
For darkness is heavy in fears
And I'm unable to lift up to my mind's eye
What I don't see of myself as yet
Let me have what I need
In this here and now
Please bring me someone
To teach me how to breathe in
The breath of life all around
So I may live freely and feel the love within
And that I may see myself again as I am
I know that now
Is the greatest moment in my life
As if I have seen sunshine
Without open eyes
If I have heard the sounds of birds
Without open ears
If I've tasted the sweetness of life
Without open mouth
If I've touched the presence within me
Without reaching out
Then I know the true one
I am to be.

Hitting the Mark

You look like a miniature angel
Standing there so still, ready to guide
Almost like a statue without a will
So quietly composed, perfect
And all I can do is drink in
What I'm thinking this moment.
Like a baby in its mother's arms portrayed
I pick up on your peacefulness so easily
Because you re the warm, soft
One, wandering for love needs so much
You appear from a distance delicate
As the thought of what is love?
Just to be in your presence is more than enough
The pleasure you give is all mine
This reciprocation is the afterglow
We leave for the shadows that follow in time
Eternity will forever evolve despite the highest gained
I only live now with nothing more for me to do
For you and I like truth intertwined inside
as an arrow passing through.

Now above It

I save the sun with all my heart
Its rays are in my lungs
I'm a little better than I was
My eyes glow white in the night my
Love tells me so
Not by moon alone but with the
Reflection—knowing my destiny
Of our own single lit star
I hear what I see mostly when
Asleep
We all live, move have our being
Outside this denseness we momentarily
Hide inside till we're caught
Behind the dreams that leads us to
The stream
Swallowed up in our own self made
Victory of one and the many
Walking along side of the endless road.
We crown ourselves with lots of paths
We take when we fail and choose
To be more than a choice beyond
Our voice
We lay and pray no more
The sun comes out and we are
Its brightness now above it.